INVESTING FOR TEENS

How To Invest and Grow Your Money!

By

Alex Higgs

Copyright 2021. Spotlight Media.
All Rights Reserved.
No part of this book may be reproduced or transmitted in any form or by any means, electronic or mechanical, including photocopying, recording or by any other form without written permission from the publisher.

ISBN: 978-1-951806-38-5

TABLE OF CONTENTS

INTRODUCTION

As adulthood draws nearer, the focus often shifts from what's right in front of you to what's farther in the future. College applications start to take up more of your time; you may be working a part-time job, and you are faced with the reality that your life is going to change after you graduate high school.

The problem is that you aren't necessarily given the tools you may need to answer some bigger-picture questions you have surrounding your finances, like how and where to invest your money. None of your math teachers likely had time to cover investment accounts like a 401k plan in great detail.

Plus, there's lots of talk about investing happening on social media right now. You've likely heard tons of discourse about cryptocurrencies like Bitcoin and DOGE that are making their way to the forefront of investment portfolios everywhere.

Gen Z has already been so impactful to the financial sector that a cryptocurrency that was based upon a meme is being legitimized before our very eyes. But nobody really talks about *how* to invest in them; they just tell you that they make lots (and lots and lots) of money doing it. So, you might find yourself wanting a little push towards your future right now to avoid some stress later on.

This guide aims to teach you about the benefits of gaining financial independence, understanding investing, and ultimately preparing yourself for a solid foundation as you make your way into the adult world. It contains everything that you need to know about finances in a reasonable amount of time. Ideally, you should be taking notes and applying the lessons learned here to your everyday financial choices. It's easy to rely on visual tools to gather all of your information, but having a written guide helps you avoid cluttered thoughts and ideas. It's all in one place here.

While it's tempting to learn everything from watching YouTube videos, resources like this guide take your learning experience to the next level. You can keep this in your pocket for future use, taking note of what you've accomplished as you continue on your journey. You also get the same high-quality, expert advice without the worry of irritating ads interrupting your retention every few minutes.

There are fewer distractions overall; if your friends text you while you're reading this guide, it won't completely thwart your progress the way it would if you were consuming video content on the same screen. The constant need to pause for advertisements or social interaction is eliminated, leaving you with only the words on this page as they guide you to financial freedom!

Beginning your journey to financial independence at a young age puts you way ahead of the learning curve. As mentioned, many people aren't given the resources they truly need because of what they do or don't have available to them in school. Personal finance classes are offered at most high schools, but they only scratch the surface. For example, you'll know how to write a check like nobody's business, but you won't have a clue about how to properly save for retirement.

So, most high school graduates are left defenseless once they get their diplomas. They're thrown into the ocean at the mercy of the sharks—only metaphorically, of course—as they start navigating the real world on their own. You've probably heard at least one adult in your life mention something that they'd wish they'd done differently "at your age." This is especially common to hear in terms of money. People wish they'd invested it more, invested it differently, or even invested it at all.

It's a tiring sentiment to hear over and over. You're like, "I get it!" The repetition feels dramatic—like they're just saying it so that you listen. But it's true;

becoming financially independent provides a drastic boost in your confidence that will get you ahead of your peers in several different ways.

Think of the feeling you get when you finally have enough money for something you've saved up for, such as a new video game console or a new summer wardrobe. You recognize that you put in tons of hours at work to get these nice things with your hard-earned money, but you keep feeling like those small checks are just not going to cut it forever. That's because it's not just about having a few hundred dollars more in your bank account! That's a small perk in comparison to the long-term benefits that financial independence can bring you.

Being financially free means that you won't have to live check to check. You'll have some left over for a rainy day or to do things that you enjoy, and you'll have valuable knowledge so that these practices are sustainable for you. Pretty soon, your peers will be turning to you for advice. You'll move through life unafraid because you'll know that you have the tools that you need for long-term success.

Many people within the younger generations are pivoting towards being small business owners instead of working for someone else. Possessing important knowledge regarding investing will provide you with the confidence you need to do just about anything. The world truly is your oyster; it's just easier to explore its waters with a few more commas in your bank account.

With that being said, you should start investing immediately if it is reasonable for you to do so. That means that you shouldn't jump into something for the thrill of it, but begin as soon as you have a foundation. Building wealth for yourself will give you a massive advantage over your peers.

Everybody starts at a different pace, and everybody follows a different path. Some people don't feel confident enough to begin investing until their mid to late thirties, and that's completely fine! However, if you have the tools and the financial means, getting a jumpstart on investing will be hugely beneficial to you, and we'll teach you everything you need to get started!

CHAPTER ONE

FAILURE: YOUR TOOL FOR A BRIGHT FUTURE

Failure is one of the most universal aspects of the human experience; however, it's one of the scariest, and most of us avoid failure at all costs. Nobody likes to feel embarrassed, but failure encourages you to want to hide in your room forever or perhaps move to a different country under a new name. There's no harsher feeling than the looming "F" on your report card after you messed up on a big exam or didn't put your all into a paper, and the results you receive reflect that.

Similarly, though, it's miraculous how quickly these hiccups can be forgotten. I've been there, too. I've cried my eyes out over what I thought was a colossal failure on my part; getting fired from jobs, failing tests, breakups, you name it! As I got older, I decided that forgetting about these failures was unproductive. Throwing them under my bed like my high school yearbooks only let them collect dust. Each failure contains a valuable lesson, and you'd be doing yourself a disservice by neglecting to acknowledge them.

I'm sure that you've heard the old saying, "The definition of insanity is doing the same thing over and over again hoping for different results." This is precisely what happens when we ignore our failures instead of learning from them. When something doesn't work, we analyze our systems until they're more productive, but we can't do that until we notice something is wrong in the first place.

For example, if you write an essay, your teacher is going to leave you some feedback. If they're a thorough grader, their feedback will be insightful, helping you to improve upon your work for future assignments. The same can be said about your career; let's say you got fired from your very first job—it happened to me—and you feel embarrassed. But you realize that you weren't compatible with that job because your skills were just different from what they needed. So, instead of applying to a similar job because it would be easy to land, you decide to apply for something that closely matches the career path you're trying to follow. That way, you'll gain experience in your desired field. If you'd applied for a job as, say, a cashier again, you likely would have hated it just as much as you did the first time. Perhaps you would have been fired again, too— not because you're incompetent, but because you're incompatible.

Some of the most successful people in the world have failed massively at various points in their careers. Imagine if someone like Walt Disney took his early failures as gospel, leaving the rest of us without the thrill of going to Disneyland for the first time and completely erasing his legacy from history. Before Mickey Mouse was imprinted into our core childhood memories, Walt Disney was told by a newspaper editor that he had no sense of imagination and a wide array of bad ideas.

That seems unfathomable for most of us today; when we think of Disney, we think of magic, adventure, and grand ideas. It's admirable that he was able to push past that failure, even admitting that he'd never lived with fear. He said, "I think it's important to have a good hard failure when you're young... Because it makes you kind of aware of what can happen to you. Because of it, I've never had any fear in my whole life when we've been near collapse and all of that. I've never been afraid."

We wouldn't have some of our most influential innovators if they'd listened to criticisms or simmered in their failures. If Steve Jobs let his pitfalls with Apple get to him, I would not be writing this book right now on my Mac. These mistakes had less to do with his skill set and more to do with his demeanor, reminding us that it's important to continue to treat those around us with kindness as we pursue success.

Jobs was rather hotheaded; many would describe him today as a major micromanager. He had to balance his perfectionism with personability. Continuing to manage Apple the way he did would have ultimately led to its total failure or a complete rebrand. It no longer would have been presented as his groundbreaking vision because he would have let his ego get the best of him. Thinking about our personal, moral failures is just as important as analyzing our career-based financial ones. The world requires us to live with a sense of balance; forgetting to act with integrity will ultimately lead to bigger failures than we should ever need to deal with.

Many wildly successful people have some serious controversies tied to their names. However, they also have a lot that they can teach us about success and failure. Mark Zuckerberg, for example, isn't necessarily popular with the general public—but his work is undeniably groundbreaking. It's difficult to remember a world where Facebook didn't exist.

When I first had internet access, it was the early 2000s. But by the time I reached middle school, Facebook swept in and completely took over everyone's digital social life. Back then, I had MySpace to lean on, but its interface quickly became dated, which is why

Facebook attempted to be revolutionary within that market. With Facebook's innovations, it became much easier and more convenient to share photos or status updates.

In Facebook's very early days, Zuckerberg tried pushing an idea called "Wirehog." It was similar to a program called Limewire, where people would pirate music files for free to transfer to their iPods or Zunes. Zuckerberg was certain that this was a million-dollar idea. He thought this aspect of his programming was essential to getting Facebook on the map, likely because of the popularity of similar MySpace features. Instead, it was a colossal failure, with the program completely shutting down in 2006 due to several lawsuits.

This must have felt entirely discouraging; creating these kinds of programs takes lots of time, energy, and money. But Zuckerberg persisted, ultimately leading to him accumulating a $28.5 billion net worth by the time he was 30. Since then, several Facebook features have tanked—except now, these blows don't reach his bank account or ego nearly as hard because he is resilient. While many criticize Zuckerberg on more personal fronts, including his responses to political events, he certainly proves that hard work pays off eventually.

We've touched on the fact that it's crucial to learn from each of your failures. But where do we begin?

How do we stomp out the anxiety that comes with messing up? It's easier than you'd think; self-reflection doesn't have to be an intimidating process. If you fail on a test, you usually look at what you did wrong, making a note to approach a similar question differently in the future. We simply must reevaluate our workflow systems, ultimately leading us to more productive habits on all fronts. Not every financial investment that you make will be a success. This is an unfortunate reality about investing, making money, and saving. Sometimes, you'll mess up.

This is especially true in terms of today's financial sector. Cryptocurrencies are exceptionally volatile. They're also quite popular and enticing to many young investors who are beginning their portfolios. You can easily purchase Bitcoin on your PayPal account, which is exciting to someone who just wants to start investing today without thinking of any potential room for error.

For example, GameStop recently caused a fiasco in the stock market as the price skyrocketed. These things are not always so publicized, but they happen frequently due to the nature of the stock market as an entity. Many people dove in due to the hype alone, hoping to make a quick buck. Some people succeeded if they got the timing just right. Others were left disappointed; they lost money as apps like Robinhood caught onto the scheme, creating difficulties for smaller investors as they were building their novice portfolios.

It did, however, teach a lot of newcomers about investment when they were previously uninterested in the topic. For many, trading stocks may have felt inaccessible unless you already had large sums of money stowed away. As a result, some people learned that they had an untapped skill, encouraging them to probe further.

I believe that it's just as important to learn where your weaknesses lie as it is to learn about your strengths. It's easy to figure out what we're good at; our egos love that stuff, taking every compliment with us throughout our days, often using it to build our senses of self. Have you ever analyzed your weaknesses, not picking them apart in a way that leads to a depressive state but thinking about them in a way that you can grow from them?

Knowing that you believe in generalized hype too easily, for example, can help you avoid some serious financial missteps in the future. Instead, you'll learn to focus on your executive skills, leaning less towards making giant investments in small startups. Being acutely aware of where you lack skills can help you build them in other areas. Nobody will be good at every aspect of anything, even investing.

Similarly, it's important not to take things too personally. This is a hard one for me, as I am very much in tune with my emotional responses to things and how others perceive me. Through the years, I've taken a step back from this as I've gotten deeper into business and investing. You build up a tough, unbreakable shell as you continue.

There's no room for heavy emotions in investment or business in general; sometimes, people just change their minds. It is that simple, even though your mind may trick you into thinking something bigger is going on. To be clear, this doesn't mean you should constantly move with a potent aura of distrust, either — people catch onto that, too. There are some people who you can trust to take your investments to the finish line, but you must build up the awareness to weed those out from the sea of wishy-washy startups.

For example, let's say Brendan puts $20,000 towards Sarah's business idea because he really, truly believes in it. He wants her to succeed as a person just as badly as he wants the idea itself to succeed. They've been friends for just around a year after they met at a tech conference in Seattle. Things go extremely well at first; Sarah is grateful for Brendan's help, consistently keeping him updated on the state of her idea. However, some months go by, and radio silence becomes their new normal. He is left frustrated, as $20,000 isn't a small amount of change. What's worse is the emotional toll it took on him. He thought his friendship with Sarah had the potential to grow into something magical as they both advanced within the business world.

In Sarah's mind, Brendan was contributing to her business knowing there are risks involved in investing. She never really promised him anything in return, except for maybe a share in her company. From a personal standpoint, though, this move felt cold. Brendan felt like Sarah was completely abandoning him, leaving him with a $20,000-sized hole in his wallet.

Instead of wallowing, though, Brendan decides to make new connections. There are always going to be exciting ideas and people in which to invest your time or money. It's simply that business is everchanging, and finances are ever-evolving. Your task is to take these failures by hand, letting them guide you to your next great venture. It takes time to get it right. You didn't learn how to draw or play guitar or football overnight; you can't expect yourself to know in what and where to invest immediately. It'll take many highs and lows, but you'll get there eventually.

CHAPTER TWO

MONEY: HOW TO MAKE IT, AND WHERE TO SAVE IT

These days, there is a massive market for making and saving money the same way that there is one for investing it. Many people believe that money is energy, therefore making it possible for money to flow through you consistently as long as you keep up the same energy on your end. Naturally, various circumstances make it difficult for people to have the same opportunities. Starting off making, saving, and investing early on in your life will put you at an extremely high advantage over your peers, regardless of the circumstances that may attempt to disenfranchise you otherwise. As long as you have a stable enough internet connection to download this book, you can make more money on your computer or smartphone alone than you probably even dreamed of.

I began my career as a copywriter accidentally, generating thousands of dollars within my first year in business from the comfort of my desk chair. Before I transferred my clients to my laptop, I was working mostly from my iPhone and library computers until COVID-19 took library access away from me.

After a quick Google search, I learned how lucrative copywriting can be if you're consistent with it. I didn't generate clients overnight; it took several months to earn more than $50 on one project. By the time I went to do my 2020 taxes, though, I realized that I had earned $6,500 in that first year. While that's not a huge amount of money, it's a big deal for someone who started writing articles on her iPhone for $10 apiece.

Options like this often require you to be at least 18 years old. This is true of freelance platforms, where they must verify your identity before you can start making money. These rules, while irritating to younger aspiring entrepreneurs, are there for your safety — making money online comes with its set of risks, just like investing.

However, there are other options available for you if you do want to pursue freelancing before you graduate high school. You can build your portfolio outside of freelance platforms, generating regular clients from people you know directly. A friend of mine used to edit books for one of her mom's colleagues, eventually leading her to complete an English degree from her local university.

You also don't have to be a writer; ask local music venues if they need photographers, ushers, or volunteers. These gigs eventually can lead to paid opportunities if you're willing to put in a little time and effort. People are also always looking for virtual assistants to do administrative tasks remotely for their businesses. This field of work has grown exponentially since the COVID-19 pandemic broke out, forcing most businesses to operate remotely.

If you're not quite at this point yet, but want to start somewhere, talk to your parents! When I was a kid, my parents helped me learn how to save money by doing petty tasks for their businesses, like shredding documents that contained personal information. This taught me the importance of routine, discipline, and goal setting. It was essentially my first job before I explored retail in high school. If you don't know any business owners, consult your loved ones about other options that you may have. It'll seem slow moving or even frustrating at first; you may see your friends working their jobs in stores while you are raking leaves or walking dogs. But as I keep saying, it's not always worth it to make a quick buck.

If your family circumstances allow, working with your parents can teach you about saving in smaller ways, too. Many of my friends' parents would take "rent" money from them each month, only to return it to them when graduation day came around. I had one friend accumulate thousands of dollars from this practice; he didn't even realize the money was leaving his checks because it was a small chunk here and there. Your parents may have tons of options for you that you didn't even think were possible—by the time you know it, you'll have reached your financial goals!

Your options don't stop or start at home. Your classmates may need help with tutoring in a subject that you're more well versed in than they are. If you offer tutoring services, you could easily make a few hundred dollars every week, and you'll be helping your peers in the process. Similarly, if you offer babysitting services, it's wise to promote these at your school if you're allowed.

Now that you have the tools you need to start making money, how do you begin saving your hard-earned cash? The first thing you'll want to do is open a simple **checking account**. These accounts typically require a small deposit to open (around $25) and won't start charging you an annual fee to keep it open until you turn 18. Some banks don't charge annual fees for checking accounts at all!

This is where all your spending money will go. It will house your income, and it will be connected to your debit card. Recently, technology has made **online banking** even easier. Many people have been ditching **big-name chain banks** and **local credit unions** for **checking account apps**. These apps are independently run, and people are drawn in by the allure of not dealing with a large corporation. While you're just starting, it's best to begin your banking journey with a traditional financial institution like a **bank** or **credit union**.

If the allure of dealing with a smaller company doesn't seem worth the risk of using a startup app, then **credit unions** might be your best bet. These are not-for-profit organizations, which often seem more personable to newcomers than big for-profit banks. I usually recommend that younger people start with the bank or credit union their parents use. Not only is it convenient, but there are often **high school** and **college checking accounts** available for you to use, no matter the banking option that you choose. These accounts are safe, easy to operate, and usually don't have an annual fee. Additionally, many of these accounts operate without **overdraft fees**, so you won't grow tempted to spend more money than you have.

Now that you know how to make and store money, how do you begin saving it? Just like **checking** accounts, **savings** accounts are available. These accounts connect to your checking account, often providing the ability to easily transfer money from one account to the other. They also come with settings that prevent you from taking too much from your savings at once so that you can reach your goals more quickly. Additionally, transfers are typically instant these days; you no longer have to wait several business days to get your money to spend on the high-ticket goal item you were saving for.

Money market accounts hold various benefits that can seriously help you further your saving habits in the long run. These accounts limit your transactions while providing you with **higher interest rates** on the funds that you store there. For this reason, many people like to use these accounts as primary savings accounts once they are well established. Many offer some of the same privileges as a **checking account**, such as check-writing and debit card capabilities. However, the downside is that the minimum balance requirement for these accounts can sometimes be a little high. They aren't always impractical for new investors, but it's important to do thorough research before committing to one. This is true of any bank account you open; always read the fine print, even if it feels like a tedious task — you'll thank yourself later!

Speaking of interest, it's crucial to get familiar with different types of **interest**. Hearing that a savings account has a **high interest rate** is great news! This means that you will make money when you aren't even thinking about it. High interest rates on credit cards are something to avoid, though, because this means that you'll lose more money every year trying to keep the card on your revolving credit. **Compound interest** is the amount that is added on top of the **principal amount** of a credit card or savings account during a certain amount of time. The **compound interest formula** is:

$$Compound\ Interest = (P(1 + i)^n) - P$$

$$P = Principal$$
$$i = interest\ rate$$
$$n = time\ period\ (i.e., number\ of\ years)$$

I promise that we won't be doing too much math together from this point on. The compound interest formula is one of the most important, practical formulas to know. Sometimes, these equations have far more value than the time devoted to them in an algebra class. Most students are immediately intrigued when money is mentioned. Some students do better on money-based units because it adds a real-world element to the problems they're solving. Understanding the compound interest formula gives a massive advantage to young investors since it's so prominent within almost every aspect of finances.

Being smart with money begins by building steady, realistic, everyday habits. This can start as small as making sure that there's always at least $50 in your checking account. That amount can increase as your dreams get bigger. Simple habits will always lead to bigger ones; if you start making your bed every day, it becomes routine, so you don't have to think about doing it anymore. The same concept applies to money. While these numbers seem big and scary when you first look at them, it's nothing that you can't manage because you earned it.

It's also important not to get so caught up in saving that you forget to treat yourself occasionally. This looks different for everyone. Some people enjoy going to concerts, some like to play sports, and others like to go shopping. Regardless of your interests, remembering to feed your soul is just as important as reaching a financial goal. Also, treating yourself will help avoid burnout. I'm not encouraging you to go overboard, but if you want a new videogame or collector's item, don't hold yourself back too much. Part of the beauty of learning how to save is learning how to spend, too.

Overall, the possibilities for young investors to make and save money are endless these days. The technological advancements that we've gone over are impressive, to say the very least, and hopefully, you have been inspired by at least one of the options that are at your disposal. I advise that you make a list of pros and cons for each option as they pertain to your situation. Not every method will work the same for each user.

For example, a beginning investor might love the idea of a money market account, only to realize that they are not yet ready to have one. Similarly, you may think you want to join your local credit union but find that a bank works better for the retail job you just got based upon your direct deposit schedule. I recommend that you also work with what's available in your area before branching out to bigger options like the independent banking apps I mentioned earlier in this chapter.

Don't let yourself become overwhelmed with saving and making money. Remember: You're likely at the very beginning stages of this journey. I always feel the need to reiterate the fact that you won't know everything all at once. This advice would have helped me so much when I was a teenager. Sometimes, the drive that teens have is consuming; they're told they must get the best grades, go to the best colleges, and create the best financial habits while they're still growing. While it's true that you should build these habits, you must remember that life is all about balance. Life isn't just a numbers game; the numbers simply help us get to the fun stuff.

CHAPTER THREE

BUCKETS: THESE THINGS HOLD YOUR INVESTMENTS

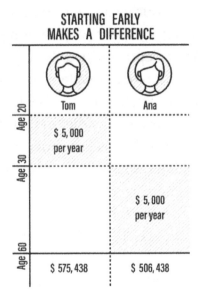

Thinking about retirement while you're still in high school is, quite literally, taxing. I remember the existential crisis that ensued when I realized graduation was near. The "real world" was looming over my shoulder the way my parents would while I was doing homework, and its voice was far more domineering than my perfectionist dad is.

I thought about retirement funds, emergency funds, and regular savings accounts like they were so far out of reach I might as well have been delusional. We were by no means poor; we simply didn't have the excessive wealth that made these discussions a natural part of my formative years. I was left to work minimum wage jobs if I wanted to have any fun during high school and college. I remain grateful for this experience; it allowed me to learn things on my own time, deepening the weight of each lesson as I learned it.

When I first started in retail, I had my regular checking account, and that was it. I was too afraid of credit cards to get one of my own. I figured I didn't make enough money to open up a separate savings account, so I kept all of my earnings in one place. This was great temporarily, as I was able to look at my direct deposits when they entered my checking account every other week on a regular schedule.

The routine helped me budget my earnings because it was so predictable. I'd generate the same number of hours on every schedule and know that I'd get the same dollar amount every pay cycle. This didn't last long, though. As my goals for saving grew larger, I began to learn about bigger-picture savings goals like retirement.

Believe it or not, people can and do begin saving for their retirement funds while they're still in high school. Right now, you're probably focused on paying for college tuition or a car. These small goals will help you in the long run. They teach you discipline when you're managing your routine income. But you need to think bigger than that, too, especially as you begin working for large corporations like retail establishments. These places may seem like unpromising, temporary circumstances, but they have a lot to offer you as you are starting to invest in yourself.

When I turned 18, my dad sat down with me to have a serious discussion about my finances. I've never really been frivolous with cash; my vice is concert tickets, and if my favorite band is touring, I'll drop several hundred dollars to see them a few times on tour. Dad explained retirement savings to me in terms of the way I saved for concert tickets. He talked about how I put aside $20 every now and then without knowing whether my favorite acts would be doing anything because I wanted to be prepared just in case they did.

I couldn't contact anyone's management companies and ask in advance to make my savings plans. I just did it automatically because I knew they'd come around eventually or release an album. Maybe I'd want to buy a merchandise bundle for it. In the long run, I'd have a bulk sum of money saved up, regardless of whether I saw my favorite band in concert that year or not.

This analogy worked wonders for me. It made retirement savings seem like less of a broad idea. I may not know when I will retire—I'm still quite young, so I have a while to go—but I do know that I've been able to start saving for retirement already because I have received such good advice. If I hadn't done this for myself, I'd be so much more stressed out later. You must do yourself a favor and start thinking about this stuff now. After working your whole life, you'd be doing yourself a disservice by not granting the future you a bit of peace by responsibly saving your money for retirement.

In this chapter, we will go over the various kinds of retirement accounts so that you can analyze which might work best for you right now. This might change over time, but knowing these terms will help you as you go along in your career. The two main types of retirement accounts fall under the categories of **qualified** and **nonqualified**. Let's dive a little deeper into them.

What is a Qualified Account?

These are some of the best known and most widely used kinds of retirement accounts. Usually, when people use "retirement account" as a blanket statement term, they are speaking about **qualified accounts**. While there are benefits to both **qualified** and **nonqualified** accounts because they both contribute heavily to your future, it makes sense that qualified accounts are more common.

Qualified accounts include plans like a 401k, which you may already be familiar with. Both qualified and nonqualified accounts include various tax benefits, and it's important to familiarize yourself with them as you begin to make your financial decisions.

Pre-Tax

It's in the name: **Pre-tax** accounts take chunks of your income before being taxed. They allow you to deposit funds before they are taxed because they hope to give you benefits from being in a different tax bracket upon retirement. Whether this bracket is higher or lower depends on several factors, all of which are personal and lead back to your career, investment choices, etc. This also provides you the benefit of reducing your current taxable income. As a result, you won't be paying a percentage of your taxes on what you make now until far off into the future. High earners love this benefit because they understand that they will likely be in a lower tax bracket by the time they retire.

IRAs

Whether or not you plan to get married in the future, it's important to familiarize yourself with the concept of **Individual Retirement Accounts (IRA)**. There are several different kinds of these accounts; some are more commonly used than others, but the biggest takeaway from learning about them should be recognizing what they can do for your financial future. Unfortunately, plans like a 401k often don't provide enough cushioning for a comfortable retirement. IRAs, however, provide the additional support that you need. This is due to multiple factors, but the most enticing of those is the fact that they allow your investments to grow quickly. Who wouldn't want an early retirement? Additionally, IRAs are either tax deductible or tax free, making their allure shine brighter as you continue to learn about them. Consult your local bank, credit union, or broker about opening an IRA.

The process will begin when you invest your money into your new account. This can come in a variety of forms like assets, stocks, and bonds. It's up to you to increase your investment over time; the amount that you contribute will allow the account to grow exponentially throughout the years. Most IRAs will feature contribution limits. Unfortunately, you cannot put an unlimited amount of money into your IRA — wouldn't that be nice, though? IRAs also have strict withdrawal rules. If you want to withdraw early, you'll be met with a fee as well as a hefty tax bill, so keep in mind that you should aim to withdraw after you turn 59 ½.

There are **four key types** of IRAs that you should get familiar with. These include **Roth, SEP, traditional**, and **SIMPLE**. Most people will qualify for traditional and Roth IRAs because these are used for individual tax filers. If you own a business or are otherwise self-employed, SEP and SIMPLE IRAs will be the right direction for you.

Benefits of an IRA

Tax advantages. All IRAs come with several tax advantages that are incredibly helpful as you continue to invest. This is especially convenient for investments like stocks and mutual funds.

They're accessible. These days, most checking, saving, and investment accounts can be opened within minutes. Several forms for opening accounts can be found online, speeding up the process even more. Additionally, you don't have to be a certain age to open or contribute to one—you just have to earn taxable income!

They are individualized. Since these accounts are completely individualized, investors are given the peace of mind that they need to know their investments are secure and, above all else, *theirs*. Several options for retirement funds, like 401ks, have the potential to make you a participant rather than an owner because they're employee-sponsored plans. With these, though, you can rest easy knowing that nobody else owns these investments but you.

Traditional IRA

A **traditional** IRA is the most widely used IRA because everybody is qualified to open one. Contributions to this kind of account are typically tax deductible. For example, if you put $5,000 in your traditional IRA that year, your taxable income will be reduced by the same $5,000 amount.

However, you don't quite get to pull a fast one on the IRS with these contributions. The moment you withdraw your funds, you will have to pay taxes on them. As I mentioned earlier, this becomes beneficial when you retire because you're likely to be in a different tax bracket. These requirements do change frequently, so it's best to keep yourself updated on the latest versions of these rules so that you're not shocked when you finally decide to open your IRA. Your goal is to always be one step ahead of the game, not behind. Just as COVID-19 changed the physical reality of our world, it also changed several aspects that we cannot see right in front of us. This includes our finances.

Generally, single filers can deduct from their IRA if their **modified adjusted gross income (MAGI)** was $66,000 or less as of 2021. Married filers have a limit of $105,000. As soon as you turn 72, you must begin to take out **the required minimum distributions (RMDs)** from your account. This is where life expectancy comes into play; depending on your life expectancy, your RMDs will differ.

If you fail to take out your RMDs, you'll receive a huge tax penalty—up to 50%! Those numbers add up quickly. Most people cower at the thought of paying the IRS 5% more than they need to, so imagine how frighteningly large of a number 50% becomes when you're earning a larger salary and making larger contributions to your IRA. That sounds like a nightmare to me! Following these rules closely helps you get the most out of your investments in the long run. Retirement truly sounds far off now, but you'll thank yourself later for being so prepared. I recommend familiarizing yourself the most with the ins and outs of traditional IRAs since many people will be opening one of them in their lifetime.

Roth IRA

Unlike traditional IRAs, **Roth IRAs** are tax free with qualified contributions instead of being tax deductible. This is where it gets a little tricky; while you can use post-tax income here, Roth IRAs can accumulate taxes on your investment gains. Since you are a young, budding investor, this is something to watch out for. Starting so young puts you at the advantage of having the most potential for investment gains. As you make your investments, be sure to carefully plan accordingly in case your gains end up being much higher than you expected at the initial start of your investment.

Once it comes time to withdraw, you can do so without facing additional income tax. There are no RMDs on Roth IRAs. Roth IRAs are great for longevity; they don't have any requirements for age as far as contributions go. People also choose Roth IRAs if they assume that their taxes will be higher by the time they get to retirement. These accounts don't let you contribute to them if you make too much money, so they're quite popular among people who predict that their tax bracket will change over time.

A major difference between traditional and Roth IRAs is that Roth IRAs cannot accept assets as contributions. You must contribute to them in cash, and the maximum amount that can be contributed to them changes periodically via IRS standards. When you choose your provider, it's important to note their fee structure. No one fee structure will be the same; these differ for almost every potential IRA provider that you will encounter. Do your research thoroughly and read the fine print. This advice is true for all investments, but a commitment like an IRA account should have a heightened emphasis on careful decision-making. Active investors tend to benefit from Roth IRA providers that offer lower trading costs and fewer fees.

Let's recap the differences between **traditional** and **Roth IRAs**:

Traditional	Roth
Anyone can open one	Anyone can open one
No income eligibility limit	MAGI can't exceed limits
No age restriction	No age restrictions
Can contribute assets	Can only contribute taxable income
Early withdrawal penalties before age 59 ½	No withdrawal penalties

While these common types of IRAs are similar, you should familiarize yourself with the differences between the two as you continue to make your investment decisions. Ask yourself questions about what you want your future to look like. Will you purchase a home someday? Do you want kids? Would you assume those kids will eventually have grandkids? These seem like far-off conditions that don't apply to you right now, but as I like to say, it's better to be one step ahead than one step behind.

As you continue to invest, your needs will change drastically. Your traditional IRA might work perfectly for you right now, but if you open a business later, you may need to change course. That's just fine; no one's path is directly linear. There will be twists, turns, and bumps along the road. If you read the fine print in every contract you sign, you'll avoid mishaps in the future if you decide to change direction. You can also have more than one retirement account open at a time, which is helpful. Just be sure that you're keeping close track of your accounts. There are also professionals, like financial advisors, who are trained to help you through this process.

SIMPLE IRA

This is where all the young entrepreneurs should get interested (no pun intended). **SIMPLE IRA** plans are wonderful for small business owners or freelancers who employ 100 people or less. The acronym SIMPLE stands for "Savings Incentive Match Plan for Employees." They're incredibly easy to set up, but it's important to know the ins and outs of this kind of account before you commit to it.

As a freelancer myself, I understand the value of a SIMPLE IRA regarding its benefits for my business should I choose to hire people along the way. Currently, it's just me, but if I ever want to hire an editing team or start an agency, a SIMPLE IRA would be my preferred choice. I've mentioned that my business began with a humble start. I started this journey accidentally; along the way, I've had plenty of ups and downs with my investments for my business because each investment I make correlates to other areas of my life in ways I may not have even anticipated.

For example, as I started generating frequent clients, I worried about retirement, healthcare, etc. Learning about different kinds of IRAs opened my eyes to the world of possibilities out there. More people are considered freelance contractors or small business owners than you might think. When I was younger, I used to be incredibly curious about how celebrities planned for retirement. They have their massive fortunes to fall back on, but where do they keep these funds secure? They likely consult with big-name financial advisors who eventually put them on the right path for selecting the IRA that best suits their needs.

Your retirement plan will likely be much smaller than that of a celebrity, though. While many young people are starting their businesses from the ground up, they are finding that they can access bigger means of success more quickly due to tools like social media. I've watched my friends get one viral video that generated sales in the thousands when previously they'd only made a few hundred per month. They've had honest conversations with me because they know I write about investment stuff, and they said our conversations about things like SIMPLE IRAs have helped them considerably through their understandable fears.

When you want to open your SIMPLE IRA, you will need to fill out an IRS form called **Form 5304-SIMPLE**.

Many people give their employees the option to choose the financial institution that hosts their SIMPLE IRA. This gives their employee a sense of freedom; as a business owner, you always want to make your employees feel comfortable at work. Employers who give their employees this choice often feel like they've added to that sense of comfort by giving employees options. This isn't a requirement, though, and it depends on how you decide to run your business. Other contributing factors may prevent you from giving employees this kind of option. On the employees' end, opening their accounts requires them to fill out a **SIMPLE IRA Adoption Agreement**.

As with all investment accounts, there are potential drawbacks that you should consider before committing to a SIMPLE IRA. These accounts won't let you save as much for retirement as an option like a **401k** plan. You also cannot transfer funds from other IRAs into this one, nor can you roll funds over from a traditional IRA without first completing a 2-year waiting period. Overall, SIMPLE IRAs are likely to be a great option for you if you are thinking of running a business that employs under 100 people. Hopefully, as your business expands, you will be well versed enough in investing that you will be able to use your knowledge to transfer your investments to different kinds of accounts as needed while considering your employees along the way.

SEP IRA

Unlike SIMPLE IRAs, **SEP IRAs** are for business owners who have few, if any, employees. These are great for single proprietorships such as mine. SEP stands for **Simplified Employee Pension IRA**. Businesses that hire employees, who are considered to be eligible participants in terms of the plan by the IRS, will need to contribute on behalf of those employees. That can get costly.

These accounts are incredibly easy to set up as well as administer. There's a high contribution limit, adding to their overall allure. You can also combine them with other kinds of IRAs, like traditional or Roth. Also, these contributions are flexible and tax deductible. However, you can't catch up to these accounts if you're 50 or over. This is an issue for business owners who start later in the game. That being said, you can combine contributions from other kinds of retirement accounts. This drawback becomes less of an issue for smart investors because they will likely have backup plans already in place. Unfortunately, there are withdrawal penalties for people under age 59 ½, but those are also quite common within other kinds of IRAs, so it's not too much of a burden for investors.

Investments like stocks are suitable for a SEP IRA because this type of account is normally placed into certificates of deposit rather than a traditional bank account. We'll talk more about stocks later, but you should make a note of this specification now so that you remember it once we get to that chapter. More young people are curious about the stock market now, especially after the GameStop fiasco, so it's understandable if that topic catches your eye.

Additionally, you'll want to plan this kind of IRA in terms of your age, your plans for retirement, and your personal risk tolerance. Those interested in stock investments tend to have a higher risk tolerance, depending on what their portfolio looks like — or what they want their portfolio to look like. As for your retirement plans, people who open these accounts a long time before retirement benefit most because they're able to diversify their investment portfolios. This practice ultimately brings better returns to your IRA since the stock market is so volatile. Let's quickly compare **SEP** and **SIMPLE IRAs**:

SEP	SIMPLE
Good for self-employed business owners	Good for businesses with 100 or fewer employees
Suitable for stock investments	Can contribute tax-deferred income
Easy to open	Easy to open
Can be combined with other kinds of IRAs	Cannot be combined with other kinds of IRAs

Good for young investors who have a long time until retirement	Contributions made by the employer belong to the employee and can be taken with them even after leaving the company
Penalties for early withdrawals	Fewer rules for both employers and employees
Typically held in a certificate of deposit vs. bank account because of withdrawal limits	Potential for the employee to choose where their account is held

Your business plan will ultimately help you curate your retirement plan. If you have a business idea now, considering the various types of IRAs will help you as you begin to plant the seeds for that business idea. No dream is too big; all dreams just need a practical plan.

401ks

My **401k** plan saved me a lot of grief when I first started working. I began working the moment I turned 16. I have always craved financial freedom, learning from an eclectic mix of adults who either had a great time saving money or a ridiculously hard time saving money. I didn't want to end up on the latter end of the spectrum, so I ended up taking the extreme route in the early stages of my working life. I've mentioned that I started in retail; my first job was working the sales floor of a massive department store that does not exist anymore. While this job was short in its term, it gave me a wonderful foundation for success in my early adult years.

For example, it was there that I learned what a 401k plan is. Most employers will offer a 401k to their employees, largely due to their accessibility and ease for the employer. The wonderful thing about a 401k plan is that you will not even recognize that money is leaving your account. These deductions are made each pay cycle, so you don't even have to think about it. Employers can also match a percentage of employees' contributions. These contributions are not taxed until employees withdraw their money.

Now that you have familiarity with IRAs, it's important to note that 401k accounts can take the form of **traditional** or **Roth**. Some people only have one or the other, and some people have both at once. That may sound confusing, but picture this: The money from your check is distributed into several different places already.

First, there's your direct deposit, which is the most exciting part, the part that you can spend (and save). Next, there are tax deductions: You don't notice those too much, but they're clearly labeled on your paystub. Then, there are the retirement deductions. If you have two different kinds of IRA accounts that hold your 401k plan, the funds simply split in those directions.

These 401k plans also can host your stock and bond mutual funds, as well as other various investments that you may own.

While 401k plans are wonderful for people who are just starting in the workforce, it's crucial to remember not to **keep all your eggs in one basket**. You don't want to have all these investments stuck in one place only to find that they are not easily accessible during an emergency. Make sure that you have other places where you can store your savings.

Other "Don't Touch" Accounts

Now that we've covered the basics, it's time to go over some other "don't touch" accounts that will be beneficial to you in the future. These accounts cover areas that you might think about less than retirement, such as your health.

Health Savings Account

It is crucial to keep up with your body. The vessel that keeps you alive requires frequent maintenance, and United States citizens are not offered free healthcare in most situations. Right now, you may have your parents' insurance, but as of 2021, you can only access those benefits until you're 26. Having a separate account for copayments is a wonderful idea that will save you from some literal headaches in the future.

For example, I had to undergo expensive dental surgery five years after I had my wisdom teeth removed. My canine teeth were severely impacted, similar to the way wisdom teeth grow in. They looked like vampire fangs! This caused lots of issues with my enamel, and I ended up needing dental implants before I turned 25. Dental work is some of the most expensive medical care available because even if you have insurance, there are many weird rules that turn certain procedures into "cosmetic" needs (e.g., veneers).

Thankfully, I planned for "just in case" medical needs and had a **Health Savings Account (HSA)** plus the option to apply for CareCredit to help with the expensive copay. However, I recommend relying on your credit score to back up health costs as little as you possibly can. Our goal is always to avoid debt whenever possible, but these avenues are great when combined with savings that you already dedicated to healthcare costs.

These savings accounts are typically pre-tax, which is helpful because you will be using the funds on an as-needed basis. Because of my dad's employment status, I was able to contribute to the family HSA. One of the only downsides to these kinds of accounts is that you must have a **High Deductible Health Plan (HDHP)** to contribute to them. However, if you are an **adult dependent** (e.g., college student), you may still contribute to the family HSA with your income. These funds roll over each year even if you don't spend them, so it adds up after a while.

Certificate of Deposit

I mentioned **certificates of deposit** briefly earlier. These bank accounts require you to have a "no-touch" period. Each term length varies based on your provider; you may have to wait three months at one institution and five years at a different one. A major benefit, though, is that CDs typically earn higher interest rates for account holders than other savings accounts.

For example, if you put $500 in your CD for one term, that $500 will grow depending on your interest rate. However, the downside to CDs is that the term length can also work against you. These are great options for earning money without even thinking about it. But if you need the cash before the term length is up, you'll find yourself stuck. I have a friend who put money into a CD the fall before they graduated college. This worked out perfectly because she planned on taking the money out post-grad, and she was able to use it towards her deposit for her first place!

Money Market Accounts

The allure of **money market accounts** begins with their versatility. They offer many of the same great benefits as the accounts I have just gone over. You have the security of CDs mixed with higher interest rates, but they usually require a much higher minimum deposit. This makes money market accounts less practical for new investors who typically have less to offer upfront. They're wonderful options if you can afford it, though; many people who have higher earnings, such as six-figure incomes, enjoy money market accounts for this reason.

What is a Nonqualified Account?

Much like several of the IRAs that we covered, **nonqualified accounts** are employee-sponsored plans. The difference, though, is that they are usually **post-tax** accounts, but we'll get to that later. They also are not required to follow ERISA guidelines, and they work best for employers who must meet specialized retirement needs.

Usually, these needs are reserved for higher-ups like executives. However, some other employees fall under this category, too. Even if you don't plan on becoming a CEO, understanding nonqualified accounts will help you as you climb the corporate ladder.

<u>**Post-Tax Accounts**</u>

Certain nonqualified accounts give investors the option to generate tax-free income after a certain period. Your contributions aren't tax deductible while you are saving, but once you retire, your overall taxable income will be reduced significantly. This kind of account usually helps people with higher incomes due to its nature.

A potential fault with this kind of account is that it will seem like more of your paycheck is going towards it as you make your contributions. However, as with all long-term investments, the benefits are plentiful once you retire. It truly depends on the career path you plan to follow, and how much you're willing to invest per paycheck.

Brokerage Accounts and What They Do

Brokerage accounts help you buy and sell your stocks, bonds, and mutual funds. These work similarly to traditional bank accounts; they offer you the option to transfer funds in and out of the account easily, especially as technological advancements continue to make this process seamless. The biggest difference between a brokerage account and a standard bank account is that you won't just be handling your money here. These accounts provide you with access to the stock market and other valuable forms of investment. Investment is the primary use for brokerage accounts.

As I mentioned, technology has rapidly expanded the range of brokerage accounts. Gone are the days where investors had to rely on costly firms. Now, you can open a brokerage account online within minutes. These accounts are a wonderful gateway for new investors. They're easily accessible, and you don't need much money to begin expanding your portfolio. Most online brokerage accounts only require that their users fund their accounts before they begin investing, but that process is typically outlined easily. There are also robot advisors with trusted AI systems that help you via complex coding.

If you are interested in investing in stocks, a brokerage account is a great place to start. This is a place that will hold these investments for you while you expand your portfolio. They can also help with long-term investments, retirement savings, and other savings goals. The brokerage is the middleman between you and your assets. Many of my friends began their financial journeys with their parents "hosting" their checking account, monitoring the funds for them so that they didn't overspend or build other irresponsible habits. A brokerage account works similarly, but the key difference is that they follow your instructions on what to trade.

Thankfully, any funds that you place into your brokerage account are also covered. The **Securities Investor Protection Corporation (SIPC)** exists to ensure that your funds are taken care of in case a brokerage firm that you trusted goes bankrupt. It's always important to remember that investing can be volatile, even if you place your funds somewhere that is otherwise trustworthy.

There are several different kinds of brokerage accounts that you should familiarize yourself with. A **brokerage cash account** works exactly the way you'd think it would. Your cash allows you to purchase stock, but you can't purchase more than what you have funded in the account. A **brokerage margin account** is like a loan, with your investments being **collateral**. What the custodian allows you to purchase will increase or decrease based on your perceived risk as a borrower.

In general, you'll want to present yourself as a trustworthy borrower no matter what you are investing in. This is a much higher-risk process than using a brokerage cash account. You're essentially using debt to invest, which can either benefit or hinder you in the long run. Sometimes, you will immediately owe the debt back to the firm that you're borrowing from. Additionally, the investments in your portfolio can be sold without notice if you end up owing more than what you have. The kind of brokerage account that you choose will solely depend on your preferences when it comes to risk and adaptability.

I mentioned that it's possible to open a brokerage account within minutes using online services or robo-advisors. However, is that option truly worth it compared to going a more traditional route? As with most things, that's up to you! While you don't want to commit to an account on a whim, you will likely know what's best for your investment portfolio.

For example, if you prefer learning as you go, online services will work wonders for you. They allow you complete freedom to invest in whatever you want, whenever you want. Robo-advisors are just that: advisors. They will provide minimal advice compared to traditional accounts that are managed by expert financial advisors at firms.

That's not to say they're unreliable. Robo-advisors certainly help; it just depends on how much advice you want. If you want to call all the shots with no additional input, online services are probably your best option. I do recommend that you consult with your friends and family to compare different options, though! People you trust will have a lot to offer you in terms of choosing where you want to host your investments.

What Is a 529 Plan?

Hopefully, you have begun discussing your plans for college with your parents. Everyone has different goals; nobody's path looks the same, and paths can change despite initial planning. Usually, though, parents think about their children's college education from the moment they are born. They want nothing more than to see their children succeed, and part of that often includes completing some form of higher education. Several factors go into this, leaving most parents wondering what they can realistically afford for their children. There are many different options for parents to choose from when it comes to preparing for their children's future.

One of these options is called a **529 plan**. This is an investment account solely reserved for education expenses. Many parents have different kinds of **college funds** that they prepare for their children, but **529 plans** are well loved for their benefits, including the flexibility and control they offer to account holders and beneficiaries. Beneficiaries can also open the account in the first place. All you need to be the beneficiary of a 529 plan is a social security or tax ID number.

Additionally, anyone can help you fund your 529 plan. My grandparents contributed a great deal to my college education. They were the account holders for my 529 plan. They understood that my parents were completing their college education when I was born, so they wanted to help however they could. I remember hearing from the very beginning of my life that I could go to any college I wanted because they were planning from the start.

This reassurance was helpful to everyone involved, and I certainly am grateful to have people in my life who cared so deeply about my success from day one. If you have not had these discussions with your family regarding any funding for college, begin immediately. They will either have a plan readily available for you, or they may be willing to work with you to start saving now. It's never too late to start saving for college. I know people who got their degrees in their thirties solely because they didn't know they could begin saving in high school! They always assumed that college degrees were reserved for people like me who had help all along; don't hold yourself back.

Furthermore, several firms allow you to have other people gift money on your behalf. This is an excellent idea for graduation gifts. These contributions go directly to education expenses, such as tuition, rent, books, supplies, tech gear, accessibility tools for students with disabilities, and other "qualified" expenses. Since this is an investment account, you can expect to receive benefits on your taxes as well as interest. Some 529 plans offer incredibly high interest rates, which is something to look for!

Firms understand that life happens; plans, people, and ideas change, which often leaves 529 plan holders wondering what will happen with the hard-earned money that they have invested. Thankfully, you can make withdrawals at any time, for any reason. It should be noted, though, that you may receive tax penalties on withdrawals for nonqualified expenses. Some people use the money in their 529 plan towards their education if their intended beneficiary chooses a different path from a traditional college route.

Work Smarter, Not Harder

Your plans should be rock-solid. Unfortunately, with any investment that you make, there will be at least some risk involved. I always say that you should "work smarter, not harder." This is especially true of investing: Strategy is key. Strategy is far more than a plan — strategies provide measurable results with detailed steps on how to achieve them. Plans feel more wishy-washy, like a to-do list that you can toss at the end of the day, only to find that you've completed maybe half of it. Time will escape you, surely, and before you know it, you'll arrive at the destination for your investment strategy, whether that be college, retirement, or both.

Teenagers today have the advantage of technology on their side. You can open a brokerage account from your iPhone in a matter of minutes if you are at least 18 and meet any other requirements that the broker has in place. While it's tempting to rush into investing immediately after acquiring all this valuable knowledge, remember that you do have time to get started. Your advantage will always be that you have this knowledge before a lot of people, placing you way ahead of the learning curve.

As always, I encourage you to talk to your family and friends about your plans. You likely have an amazing team of people there that have always wanted to see your success. Now, your job is to go forth and conquer responsibly!

CHAPTER FOUR

THE SAND: WHAT YOU CAN FILL YOUR BUCKETS WITH

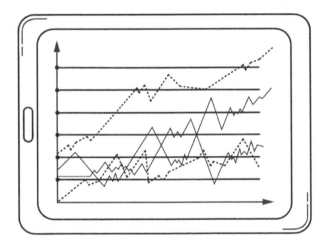

If you have any social media presence at all, you have likely been hearing lots about the stock market ever since it made headlines in early 2021. Because it's become so easy for anyone to open a brokerage account, a new wave of investors has begun exploring the stock market and the ways that they can build their portfolios.

Gone are the days when the benefits and losses of the fluctuating stock market were reserved to brokers in suits and ties at Wall Street. The people around me have begun discussing investment for the first time, asking me for advice wherever I can offer it. It's wonderful that so many people are inspired to take strides for their future. Making the market more accessible is a great thing as it opens opportunities for everyone involved.

However, there are several things that you need to know to get started. When I was in 8th grade way back when, I played what was called the Stock Market Game. This was a simulation that my teacher created to give us a head start — similar to what I am providing you in the contents of this book — except we received a grade in the Stock Market Game. I believe other schools around the country run similar exercises, allowing their students to explore what seems to be far in the future, planting seeds in their minds as they transition to high school.

Ironically enough, my team lost the Stock Market Game. I am talking about complete, utter failure! If this had been real money, we would have taken a huge hit to our wallets and assets. Thank goodness it was all play, right? We didn't get a failing grade on the assignment because the goal was not just to win but also to reflect. Our saving grace was the fact that we could all write a good essay. Now I'm writing books on investing; ironic, isn't it?

Stocks

So, what *are* **stocks**, anyway? Stocks are a lot of **shares**, which are investments that culminate into ownership of a company, all divided up by whoever holds these investments. Many see stocks as an easy way to build wealth, which is only partially true. There's much more that goes into it, though.

People make money in stocks if the company they're investing in is doing well. That's why beginners often opt to buy stocks in well-known companies since the assumption is that these brands will continue to do well. If a company is big enough, like companies that are known worldwide, people often assume that their stocks will still reap rewards for them during times of economic crisis. Many people often find a thrill in the fact that they can hold ownership to some of these wildly popular companies, allowing them to grow their financial status through well-strategized investing.

People make money from investing in stock because they are essentially buying into a company's success or loss. That's why many feel that it's smart to choose trusted brands that they know will be successful for a long time to come. Other people enjoy the risk that comes with investing in companies that they just feel are "right" for them, ultimately ignoring certain red flags. This includes people buying into startups or cryptocurrencies like Dogecoin, which we'll discuss more later. While there are benefits to this process, you must remember how volatile the stock market is. You may feel an urge to "hold the line," as people say, or sell if you feel a potential loss pending. The final call is up to you!

The Value of Stock

The value of a particular stock rises or falls for many reasons. These include hype, product recalls, or poor communication on a company's behalf, leading to customers avoiding business with them if their values are not being respected.

The GameStop fiasco was possible solely due to hype. Before the incident was newsworthy, it was circulating the internet at a rapid speed. What started as a bunch of Reddit users joking around became national news—not to insinuate that this is the first time that's happened. We all know the power that Reddit holds. The number of people who opened brokerage accounts because they wanted to buy stock in GameStop is mind blowing. Some saw wonderous amounts of success from all this while others took losses. That's simply how the game works; you just have to play with enough strategy to keep up.

Stock traders need to regulate their emotions when it comes to their investments. There will be high-stress situations, such as unexpected losses, that will leave you feeling frustrated or overwhelmed. You must remember that you chose these companies for a reason. You understand their worth, and you understand that a momentary headline may be screaming of doomsday when that is far from the truth. Many professional investors advise that you only check on your stocks once per quarter. This strategy helps you avoid making knee-jerk decisions based on emotions and temporary setbacks, leaving you to properly strategize without any distractions.

Similarly, writing pros and cons lists will help you during anxiety-inducing times. Many people keep a journal that is reserved for their investments. It may seem silly to write diary entries regarding your portfolio, but this will help you ease your mind. A calm mind is necessary for successful investing because clutter will show in your losses as much as your gains.

The goal for investment is always to see a return. This cannot happen if you put your cash in on a whim or you let your anxiety get the better of you. I feel as though a lot of advisors neglect the emotional elements of investing. We often picture figures like "The Wolf of Wall Street" who only care about their money. That is simply not the case for most people; most of us work incredibly hard for our earnings, and the thought of losing it when we were attempting to gain is enough to give anybody a panic attack — or nightmares, at least.

Letting it Simmer

Time is your best friend as an investor. A common misconception is that timing is the secret to successful investing, but learning to let things simmer will take you even farther. You can indeed make a few dollars from stocks on the same day of your initial trade. This isn't recommended, though, because of factors such as interest. Many experienced investors will let their stocks sit there for decades without selling them. That's a wild thought for most of us, considering most people start off investing small amounts. Waiting a decade to see a return sounds ludicrous to the average investor.

You can strategize with a few techniques; firstly, the **dollar-cost** average will help you immensely. Many online brokerage accounts allow automatic investments to be made on a schedule that is chosen by their account owners. This requires a bit of thought, as you'll need to ensure that you always have the funds ready in the deposit account that's linked to your brokerage account.

But with enough practice, you'll be able to accurately time your investments to get the highest return. The predictability of at least knowing when you will make your investments eases a lot of people's minds. You can't control how stocks fluctuate, but you can control when you invest in them, ultimately leading you to make better financial decisions overall.

Keep Your Eggs in Many Baskets

Avoiding putting all your money in one place will help, too. When I first bought my stock, the thought of losing out on my first try was soul crushing. I couldn't handle a major loss as a college student; investing in anything was risky enough, and at times I wondered if I was in over my head, only leading to trouble down the road.

Naturally, this was not the case, and my anxieties eased over time. What helped me greatly was when I started dividing my investments into thirds instead of dropping a load of cash into one spot. Even if a company looked promising for my investment, I understood there was a chance that it could fail or that I could lose money on a smaller scale.

So, instead, I picked three different companies, investing one-third of my initial amount into each. This ended up being a total success for me because each company that I chose did well. I was able to make enough money for my next semester of college just by those investments alone. To be clear, I'm not encouraging you to do this to pay for something on a deadline. However, stocks have helped me understand the importance of dividing my investments.

Ultimately, your best friend in the stock market will be the experience that you earn as you go. You won't become an expert overnight, and it's not as easy as throwing some of your paychecks into a savings account. There's a lot of thought that goes into it, but you'll figure it out before you know it. Soon enough, you'll be impressing your parents at the dinner table with all your stock market knowledge!

Bonds

An episode of a TV show I loved as a kid used **bonds** as the punchline for a bit. One of the characters was thrilled to find out that his parents gave him bonds for his birthday because they announced it in the form of $1,000. These kindhearted parents invested $1,000 on their child's behalf, knowing that it would grow to something much larger someday.

This wasn't so thrilling for the teenager since he wanted instant gratification from getting $1,000 for his birthday. I'm sure he thanked them when he was older—well, I hope he did! He could have made a serious profit from that helpful but hilarious birthday gift.

Most likely, the bond that was purchased for this 14-year-old would have yielded an exceptional amount of wealth by the time he turned 18. Bonds increase in value with **maturity**. That is, the longer people hold onto their bonds, the more profit they will likely see. Of course, maturity isn't the only contributing factor to a bond's value. However, it's the one most people know and understand when they are first learning about bonds.

How Bonds Work

Bonds are a valuable but volatile investment. Some argue that bonds are even more volatile than stocks because it's often easier to generate an idea of when a company will succeed or fail. With bonds, you must consider factors like the economy, especially if your bond was issued by a government institution. That's right: Government institutions can issue bonds to investors if they need funds for projects such as roads.

Typically, bonds are either issued by **governments** or **corporations**. For example, let's say a major corporation is looking forward to its next product launch. They determine that they will benefit from expediting the launch of this product but need a little bit of financial help to do an early release. If they release their product early, they will either meet or exceed their sales goals instead of potentially missing them due to poor project management. Even the best companies fall short on their strategies sometimes! This is, of course, since all corporations are still run by humans. AI has not gotten that smart yet.

So, the company issues bonds to investors with the idea that the early release of the product will generate profit for both the investor and the company. This process allows investors at many levels of experience to be lenders, which often helps them in the future as they need to take out loans of their own.

You always want to be the lowest risk possible for people who are going to invest in you, and vice versa. You'll see that bond issuers need the loan to repay debt, too; it's not just a loan for their ongoing operations or quarterly/yearly sales goals that would fall flat without this extra help. Bonds are either traded publicly or **over the counter (OTC)**, depending on the circumstances. It is more common to see public bond trades versus OTC ones.

Since bonds are issued from government institutions or corporations, they are the ones responsible for repaying this loan. The investor makes money from the interest that is added to these payments. If the bond has a longer **maturity date,** or date at which the bond must be fully repaid, it will likely make investors more money.

The interest rate for bond payments is referred to as the "**coupon rate**." I'll explain that in more detail later. Bonds run at **par** for a face value of anywhere from $100–$1,000. The teenager from the show I used to love was lucky that his parents invested a sum of $1,000 into a bond for him with the idea that it would mature with time.

Commonalities Between Bonds

There are four common characteristics that bonds share. **Face value** is exactly what it sounds like. This is the amount that the bond is going to be worth once it reaches maturity. Also, this is the amount that issuers use as they calculate their interest payments. If an investor buys a bond, they will receive the face value after it matures, and its value or loss will change as it matures.

Earlier, I mentioned a coupon rate. This is the bond issuer's interest rate that they pay to the lender. The higher the interest rate, the more money that bondholders will make from their investment. For example, if a bondholder purchases a bond with a 10% interest rate at $1,000, they will receive $100 payments from the issuer each year until the debt is paid.

Do not confuse coupon rates with **coupon dates**. These are the interest payment dates for the bond issuer. These change circumstantially with the standard being semiannual payments. A bond's **maturity date** is when it will mature, and the bondholder gets its face value from the issuer. Finally, its **issue price** is the amount that the bond is initially sold for from the issuer.

Unlike regular loans, it is the companies that are getting their credit rating checked. Their credit quality will reflect that level of trustworthiness. Companies provide risk to you as an investor instead of vice versa as you are likely used to. Bonds do not follow credit reports from bureaus that you are familiar with, such as TransUnion or Equifax. Instead, they gather their data from **Standard and Poor's**, **Moody's**, and **Fitch Ratings**. **High yield** or **"junk"** bonds are those that are riskier and will gather a much higher coupon rate to compensate for the added risk.

Managing Risk Factors

While you continue to expand your investment portfolio, you will learn just how important risk factors are when you are making decisions. You should never invest on a whim, but you must also learn how to trust your gut. Your intuition will develop with time.

In the case of buying bonds, you have the exact opposite problem that you usually do as an investor. The first time I bought a bond, it threw me for a loop for this very reason. You're used to being the cause of risk for lenders. Now, you *are* the lender, so the responsibility is on the company or the government that's borrowing from you. You don't have the same risks that are present in the stock market, but the losses can be just as grand if you are not careful. Therefore, it's imperative to calculate your values as an investor when you are putting your money into something. I'm not necessarily speaking on ethics, but mostly in terms of your values when it comes to business and what it means to see success. For example, if a company seems promising and you want to buy a stock or bond, I won't tell you not to just because the company isn't highly developed yet. But you must know the game to play it well.

When it comes to bonds, they change in value according to their **duration**. This is the sensitivity with which their interest rate changes depending on factors like the economic climate. Many new investors get this term confused with a bond's "maturity." They are not the same; duration, in this case, is not measured solely as a time value. It is more closely linked to price values. A bond's **convexity**, or rate of change for its duration, is hard to calculate and is usually determined by seasoned professionals.

Categories of Bonds

Bonds are separated into four main categories: **corporate**, **municipal**, **government**, and **agency**. Corporate bonds are those that are issued by businesses. These corporations seek help from investors under the impression that they will save money due to the market's more favorable rates. This allows companies to avoid taking out a business loan and facing potentially higher interest.

A government bond might be issued by the U.S. Treasury, for example. These bonds are referred to as **"bills"** or **"notes."** You may have heard of the term sovereign debt in a government class at school. This is referring to bonds issued by national governments. An agency bond is issued by a government-affiliated organization.

Two of the most popular are **Fannie Mae** and **Freddie Mac**. They were created by Congress with the hope that they could bring more stability to the mortgage market. The goal is that by inviting investors who might not have otherwise put money into mortgages, these bonds can provide liquidity.

Varieties of Bonds

Just like there are four categories of bonds, there are also four varieties available to most investors. **Zero-Coupon** bonds are exactly as they seem; they do not issue coupon payments, but rather get a discount on interest under the rule that they will pay their lender, the holder of the bond, in full.

Convertible bonds are another option. These bonds allows bondholders to transform their debt into stock after a while, depending on various factors like share price. It's almost like turning water into wine. Well, not quite, but it sure is a nice option. Companies enjoy this type of bond because they know they might save some money in the long run if they find a lender who is willing to convert their bond to stock. The downside for investors appears when the company's project turns out to be a failure. They don't get the additional cushioning that they typically would from coupon payments from their borrower.

A **callable** bond presents investors with far more risk. Issuers have the power to call it back as its value is fluctuating, and naturally, they will try to save money wherever possible, leaving the bondholder at a disadvantage. Alternatively, investors are presented with sparkling interest rates because the bonds are inherently riskier for lenders. They wouldn't want to completely turn investors away with the scarier factors that are involved with callable bonds. They still need the money, after all. Therefore, they need to offer something, and the easiest thing for them to offer their investors is interest.

Puttable bonds give investors the option of selling them back before the bonds have fully matured. Let's put it in perspective: If an investor puts $1,000 in a project they feel might fail, this allows them to reduce their loss at the end of it all. I spoke earlier about intuition. This is where it comes in handy. You may find yourself wanting to invest in something just because you are passionate about it. We've all been there!

Options like puttable bonds may relieve some anxieties while still being realistic about the fact that there's risk involved. Issuers understand that investors benefit from this; in return, they receive a lower coupon rate. Sometimes, this option exists with the only intention being to entice lenders to buy the bond. Always make sure you read the fine print.

Yield-to-Maturity Rate

For this next section, we need to do some more math. The **yield-to-maturity (YTM)** rate is a useful formula for understanding a bond's price. This number is a bond's anticipated **return**, which is determined under the notion that it will be held until it fully matures. The TYM rate is notated as an annual rate.

This formula may confuse new bondholders. However, much like with a high school algebra class, this formula gets easier to use as you practice it. If you take a personal finance class, you might get a little more hands-on experience with this formula. I remember that we did some practice rounds with it, and I eventually saw it on a quiz later on. In high school, I did much better in math when it was focused on finances. The real-world applications allowed me to memorize formulas much quicker than things like the Pythagorean theorem.

$$YTM = \sqrt[n]{\frac{Face\ Value}{Present\ Value}} - 1$$

Thankfully, some calculators help us with these formulas. Many online calculators provide easy access to the YTM formula, allowing you to input data quickly without getting too consumed by numbers and fractions.

How to Buy Bonds

Similar to stocks, bonds can be purchased from brokers. You have options depending on your needs. Both **full-service** and **discount** brokers being available. Bonds have become much more accessible due to technological advancements. There are online brokers, just like those for stocks, that can help you get started with bondholding.

The internet is a wonderful thing; investment previously felt like a practice reserved for the ultra-wealthy. Every day people had their financial dreams limited to income that they could generate from a salary. Now, though, the options feel limitless. I know friends who downloaded an app just to check it out, and they found themselves with a budding stock portfolio within a week.

Always make sure that you are going through trusted brokers. Where there are a thousand new, legitimate opportunities to profit from investing, there are bound to be several misleading outlets. Make sure to do thorough research before you commit to any financial institution or broker.

Understanding stocks and bonds are key elements to your overall success with investing. These assets are some of the easiest ways to begin growing your portfolio. Furthermore, the accessibility with which these assets are available to you is certainly alluring, drawing many new investors to them right from their start. Regardless of what you decide to put your money into first, you want to make sure that you're investing in something that you believe in. With stocks and bonds, you can directly contribute to companies and causes that speak to your heart.

CHAPTER FIVE

HOLES: THESE THINGS CAN EAT AWAY AT YOUR MONEY

Any investment that you make will come with an element of risk. Hopefully, you will have learned so much about which investments work best for you that your risks will be limited. However, every single investor will experience some consequences when it comes to their investments. These losses don't always have to be severe. Some losses are rather small and some are tremendous, but all of them are learning opportunities. You're smart enough to know that all your actions come with consequences, for better or worse. Your financial decisions are no different.

I didn't know this when I was a teenager, but I was setting myself up for being an investor when I began purchasing collectibles from my favorite bands, film franchises, and tv shows. These things can generate a lot of value over time (just like stocks and bonds). What makes collectibles even more valuable as an investment is the fact that most people who actively seek them out belong to a niche demographic.

Usually, people interested in putting giant chunks of change into that sort of thing are superfans. So, as I was collecting vinyl records when I was 16, I was doing so for the fun of it without realizing that some of my records would be worth hundreds of dollars by the time I reached 25. That timeframe isn't huge either in terms of maturity—it hasn't even been ten years! But some of my most favorite records are valuable to people just like me. So, we're willing to invest in them while giving the item's owner a serious profit.

Unfortunately, not all my personal investments in collectibles ended up generating that much value. There are some records and T-shirts that ended up being incredibly commonplace within the community. Additionally, there are people on the internet who make fake versions of these items in hopes that they can generate a profit, too, thus reducing the overall value of the original item.

Thankfully, most of my items are worth so much to me that I don't care about returning a profit from them. If I found myself in a pinch someday, though, I could live with the comfort that I had at least a few valuable items to help me bounce back. Such is the case with anything you invest in; you can't be certain that you will gain a massive profit from it, but you can make smarter choices when you understand the potential risks that come with your financial decisions.

Types of Risks

There are several kinds of risks that come with investing. They typically fall under categories that are easy to follow, allowing you to remember them without having to think too deeply about them. There are four common categorizations of investment risk.

Inflation

The term **inflation** refers to the amount by which an economy's price level increases with time. I'm sure that you have heard your parents or guardians discuss inflation at some point. The value of a dollar changes as years go on.

Your investments might lose their **purchasing power** over time due to inflation risk. Sometimes, for several different reasons, you won't be able to accurately predict this change. The economy can prove to be quite volatile, leading to drastic changes very quickly. You just might not be able to see those coming every time they occur.

We know that bonds increase in value with their maturity rate. But what happens when inflation takes a toll on that? Let's say that you purchase a bond because it offered a shiny coupon rate, one that you just couldn't pass up. Then, the economy takes a serious hit because of a giant surge in demand for major goods, like oil, that no one predicted. The inflation rate goes up 11% that year. This leaves you at a loss because your coupon rate is now worth much less than it was when you purchased the bond. You can't do anything about it either since the terms of your bond cannot be changed at this time.

Don't fret, though; almost every potential risk factor can be countered with some strategizing. Remember: Strategy is far more than a plan. When you strategize, you think of the long-term consequences versus short-term goals. Even though the inflation rate might not be entirely predictable, you can estimate and use that estimation to your advantage.

Inflation premiums are a useful tool that can help you do just that. For example, as you are creating the terms of a new bond that you're purchasing, you can add a premium to the coupon rate that might match the inflation rate that is current at the bond's maturity date. If you assume that the inflation rate will increase by 5%, be sure to add that 5% premium to the terms of your bond. As a lender, you must give yourself that element of protection.

Market

An incredibly impactful risk factor that you should consider when you are expanding your portfolio is **market risk**. This is one of the most volatile types of risk due to its overall nature. The entire market is impacted by market risk, therefore leaving individual investors at a bit of a crossroads when they are strategizing their investment moves.

It would be too simple to think of market risk as the end-all to your investment decisions. Why would you choose to put your money into something that could be so harmful if you are not careful? Thankfully, as with all kinds of risks, there are ways to combat market risk and its influence on your portfolio, especially if you study the various components that give it the potential to be dangerous.

Market risk is also known as **systematic risk**. In many cases, risk factors can be minimized when you diversify your portfolio effectively. We have discussed the importance of diversification several times; however, it is unfortunately not the ultimate solution to every potential problem you'll face as an investor.

It's important, but things like systematic risk need to be combated in other ways to minimize their effects on your finances. You can't control events like recessions or severe political unrest, but you can prepare yourself for them! But why is market risk such a big deal? Market risk is a heavy hitter to investors because it exists due to price changes.

In college, when you take a statistics class, you will learn about **standard deviation**. Standard deviation is the measurement of the variation in a set of values. Prices of things like stocks change frequently, leading to the **volatility** of the investment in its entirety. This volatility is calculated annually, usually expressed in a whole value like $5. It is also expressed as a percentage like 15%. Thankfully, there are a few protections set in place for investors when it comes to market risk.

All companies that are publicly traded must disclose their potential risk factors. This includes elements like productivity levels that impact their overall sales per quarter. The **Securities and Exchange Commission (SEC)** requires this of companies so that investors have a comprehensive look into what they are putting their money towards. For example, you'll know from these disclosures if you align with a company's values on a basic moral level. Likewise, if they engage in trade policies you don't like, you'll know right away. Moreover, you'll be able to see what potential risks come with investing in their brand.

There are three main kinds of market risk:

- **Interest rate risk** is exactly what it sounds like. Interest rate fluctuations are volatile and can be affected by seemingly small events like when banks announce policy changes. Bonds are typically affected by this kind of risk.
- **Commodity risk** is impactful to things such as oil or corn. These resources are in incredibly high demand, but their risk factors are due to things that cannot be controlled.
- **Currency risk** occurs during price changes regarding different currencies in relation to each other. This kind of risk mostly affects people who hold investments in other countries. This is also known as **exchange-rate risk**.

The **value-at-risk (VaR)** method is a statistical risk management tool that can help you predict the potential loss of a stock portfolio. It also can help you calculate a more detailed probability for that loss occurring. This method is flawed but helpful; it can't perfectly predict long-term measurements for your bigger investments.

However, it can save you lots of time, money, and heartache on short-term ones. Sometimes, the short-term investments are the ones that novice investors get set on because they feel as though a quick gain could lead to something more. Tools like the value-at-risk method eliminate your rose-colored view by giving you a realistic perspective of what you're doing.

I don't want to scare you away from investments like bonds because market risk exists. Think of all the people who would have missed out on some serious gains if they lived in fear of potential risks. There are so many new and seasoned investors who have learned through trial and error. No one's experience will be equal to their neighbor's; it's up to you to find what matters to you. If you have the drive, you'll surely find success somewhere regardless of potential risk.

Liquidity

The **Global Financial Crisis (GFC)** rewrote everybody's standards for investing and the ways in which risk can present itself. This crisis began in 2007, with the United States recovering recently in 2016. By now, the crisis seems like a thing of the past for most families. Many have fully recovered and found blossoming careers and stable lifestyles even after such a drastic global economic event.

Not everyone was so lucky, though. There are still people who are recovering from the effects of the crisis after taking such huge losses that their lives were completely altered. It is looking up these days, with many people making smarter, less impulsive decisions that ultimately culminate in better financial health for most working-class people.

The crisis was sparked by some terrible investment decisions on everybody's behalf. Borrowers were biting off more than they could chew, taking out home loans that were far beyond their reasonable means of repayment. Lenders weren't doing much to fact check, approving many borrowers for these loans without realizing the risk on their end of doing so. People were buying property with the intention of "flipping" homes so that they could return a profit. All the above resulted in a mass number of missed repayments, impacting both borrowers and lenders. Moreover, foreign countries wanted a piece of the pie during the giant housing boom that took place before the market crash. This led to even bigger losses and an entire Global Financial Crisis.

This event focused everyone's attention on the concept of **liquidity**, which was something people didn't think much about before the crisis. An asset's liquidity is the ease at which it can be resold into a market. **Cash flow risk** ensures that borrowers can fund any potential liabilities that they may have. Many people hold credit cards, which would come with cash flow risk. This kind of risk is also known as liquidity risk.

Market risk is a more prominent concern with assets such as houses. Properties that once held high market value might not do so well in poor conditions like the huge crash in the housing market after the GFC. Liquidity risk usually occurs because of time or lack thereof. Careful strategizing and monitoring of your cash flow and assets can help you reduce the chances of being subjected to harmful effects from liquidity risk.

The VIX

Since volatility is such a major player in most investors' strategies, it's crucial to understand each method that's used to measure it. We've discussed a few of these, but it goes even deeper. Tools like the **Cboe Volatility Index (VIX)** help us measure the projected strength of some near-term price changes of the **S&P 500 index (SPX)**.

This real-time index provides projections that are 30 days forward. Basically, the VIX helps us calculate the level of fear that investors have at that moment. These fear levels will fluctuate constantly, but it's up to you to use them to your advantage or loss, as with anything else.

The "Fear Index" and You

If there is one universal truth that exists between all humans, it is that we are predictable creatures of habit. If there is another, it is that we operate largely on emotional terms. That is, we allow our emotions to govern our actions in many instances. Believing that emotions do not play a role in large financial decisions would surely be a naïve mindset to live by. Money makes us do all kinds of things. We use money to build our homes, to put clothes on our backs, and to fund our passions. When we feel that something will threaten the security of our finances, we panic. Panic creates several different kinds of reactions on its own, too.

As a result, CNNMoney created what is referred to as the **Fear and Greed Index**. This index exists under the premise that investors largely operate via means of fear and greed, as its name suggests. Fear might lead investors to sell their investments too quickly, and greed holds the opposite effects. The Fear and Greed Index allows investors to see measurable terms of where everybody is emotionally in that moment. Many people use it to make decisions regarding things like their stock portfolio, but others see it as a tool to measure how the market is doing in its entirety. Regardless, the index exists to benefit you, but it's all a matter of willingness to use it on your behalf.

People who are emotionally aware of themselves have a deeper understanding of their emotional patterns than others who are more detached. This understanding also gives them the ability to predict their reactions to higher-stakes emotions, such as when money, and large sums of it, are involved. For example, if you struggle with anxiety but still want to invest in the stock market, the Fear and Greed Index might help you behave rationally when you're unsure due to your emotional state.

Regardless, there will always be some element of fear when you make an investment. You can't let it stop you, though; you should only let it guide you. Our intuition exists to help us get through sticky situations, and you'll find that it's often right. The Fear and Greed Index will simply help you determine what your intuition is saying and what's not.

Taking the journey to financial freedom certainly has its ups and downs. It is a balancing act when it comes to managing money, and it can be overwhelming to those who have never handled money in these quantities before. You must check in with yourself at various points of your financial journey to ensure that you're remaining levelheaded. Your mental health always matters, and that is no different when you are thinking about your finances. I had a very difficult time with this when I first started.

There were times that I remember checking my bank account only to fall into a panic attack moments later because I thought I had messed up. It seems so finalized in the moment because you can't reverse a purchase that easily. Sure, items can be returned, but impulses can make you do things you regret later. However, I formed a routine with myself that I swore not to break, and it has been completely game changing!

For every small investment that I made, like the purchase of a small stock, I would schedule a time when it would be okay for me to buy something just for fun. While beginning your investment portfolio at a young age does come with more benefits than disadvantages, you must remember that you're still young! Don't hold yourself back from things you love just because you have certain goals to meet.

Fear will guide us, and fear will distract us. Fear is so impactful to humans that an entire index has been created to measure the amount of fear in financial markets. However, the difference between a good investor and a great investor is that a great investor will use their fear to their advantage, whereas a good investor uses it purely for prevention. The choice is yours!

CHAPTER SIX

CREDIT: HOW IT CAN HELP, AND HOW IT CAN HURT

The concept of **credit** was so frustrating to me when I first started out. This is likely to also be true for teens. How can one build credit if you need credit to build it? It seemed like a dead-end street, and I wanted a way out before I was granted a way in.

Of course, I was a dramatic teenager, after all. I thought that not getting approved for a credit card from my favorite retailer was the end of the world when I turned eighteen. I didn't realize the implications that came with giving a recent high school graduate that kind of responsibility. In hindsight, I wasn't ready for it, either. I would have made tons of avoidable mistakes.

Conversely, some people avoid using credit like it's the plague. They believe that having no credit is better than having bad credit, and one fell swoop will surely impact their credit score beyond repair. Those people are incorrect, but the fear is incredibly understandable, especially given the fact that it still takes some digging if you are seeking accurate information on credit building or repair.

Unfortunately, the American high school system has not made many strides when it comes to teaching this concept to its students. I got a little bit of information on credit in the personal finance class I took during my senior year, but it was not comprehensive. Thankfully, there were influencers I followed a few years later who sparked my interest (pun intended) in the subject, leading me to create healthy credit habits as soon as I could. I never ended up getting that credit card from my favorite retailer, though. This is probably for the best.

What *Is* Credit, Anyway?

Your **credit** score refers to the level of trustworthiness that lenders assume you have based upon a points system. Credit scores range from 300 to 850, with 300 being the worst and 850 being the absolute best. Several different credit bureaus provide you with a credit score depending on your overall history.

The Credit Bureaus

There are three major credit bureaus, and your score will be different across each of them. That's frustrating, I know, but as long as you are responsible with your lines of credit, it won't matter too much. These bureaus are:

- **Equifax**—This bureau suffered a blow to its reputation in 2017. As a result, they now offer a free tool for people to check their scores if their information was compromised.
- **TransUnion**—This bureau got its start in 1968. Originally, it was a holding company for a car tank company. These days, people recognize it as one of the three major bureaus, and it is widely trusted.
- **Experian**—This bureau uses FICO 8 to calculate people's scores. It also provides a "boost" option that allows users to connect things like their cell phone bill to their credit score for free with the hope that timely payments will boost their score.

FICO

Essentially, your **FICO** score, established by **Fair Isaac Corporation**, is the number that most people would recognize as their credit score. This is the three-digit number that will summarize the findings on your credit report. A FICO score above 670 is generally seen as good by most standards. You will probably see terms like **FICO 8** or **FICO 9** to describe your trustworthiness and determine the interest rate that you are likely to get. FICO 8 is used across the three major bureaus.

The History of Credit

Credit scores were established in the 1950s by Bill Fair and Earl Isaac. Together, they made the Fair Isaac Corporation. Before the invention of credit, it was difficult to determine a person's worthiness. This often led to bad deals on all ends, with people biting off more than they could chew and lenders losing out due to missed repayments. The idea of a standardized system was great in theory; if everyone was measured the same way, it would be easier for people to live within their means and only borrow what they could afford to pay back.

However, the system started with some basic inequalities. While Fair and Isaac had wonderful intentions at the beginning, factors such as race and gender impacted people's credit score and whether they could hold a line of credit at all. Women couldn't hold a line of credit until 1974, when the late Supreme Court Judge Ruth Bader Ginsburg voted for women to have the ability to have a credit card.

The racial implications are less overtly present, but they are there nonetheless. The system was supposed to be unbiased, but that doesn't stop those who believe people of color are less responsible than white people. Thankfully, many strides have been made in that regard, and people are less likely to have their credit impacted by factors such as race, gender, and sexuality.

The way that we determine a person's "worthiness" in financial terms is likely to grow more progressive with time. Gen Z tends to have a higher understanding of how marginalized groups are impacted by financial matters. As they continue to hold positions of power, the current systems for managing and building credit will likely change. For now, though, the methods that are currently in place are expanding for the better. But where do you start?

Your Credit History

Right now, you probably do not have a credit score. That's right—you probably do not have a credit score, even if you are eighteen. There's very little chance that any financial decisions you have made thus far would have impacted your credit score. That's great news; you have a clean slate, and you can easily achieve the score you desire... and manage it!

However, it does come with a few disadvantages as far as the options you will have when you are opening your first line of credit. Don't get discouraged, though. It is easier than ever for young adults to begin using credit lines responsibly.

Opening a Credit Card

Earlier, I mentioned the frustrations that come with not being able to open a credit card if you don't have a credit score at all. These days, it's easier than ever to open your line of credit and use it responsibly. **Secured credit cards** are a wonderful place to start. You can open a secured credit card through most major banks, and I recommend going with one from the bank that hosts your checking account.

These cards are wonderful for new borrowers because they hold you responsible for your spending as soon as you open them. You put a deposit down, and that deposit acts as your line of credit. It can increase depending on your responsibility level, but it mostly stays at the amount that you deposited when you opened the account. The best part about secured credit cards is that you can start with as little as $200! I recommend using a credit card for recurring bills like your monthly Spotify or Netflix payment, but nothing huge.

As I mentioned earlier, a major retailer that I love offers a credit card that provides an incentive for its customers. This is true with many major retailers; they'll give you discounts such as 5% off each purchase that you make with the card. While I don't hate the idea of store credit cards, I advise that you approach them with caution.

These cards are an admittedly awesome marketing strategy. You already have your brand's superfans interested enough in your services and products to spend their money at your establishment weekly or even daily, so getting them to apply for a credit card is a no-brainer. The downside is that they typically come with a higher interest rate, leaving their users stuck with a higher bill than they normally would have at the end of every month. My biggest advice when choosing a store credit card is to check the benefits in comparison with the interest. Would 5% savings on each purchase make a big enough difference after interest is calculated?

Another popular kind of credit card is offered by major airlines. Many people opt to get credit cards from airlines that they favor because they offer free miles with regular purchases. This means that a trip to the grocery store can eventually lead you to visit Bali.

That sounds great, doesn't it? These cards occasionally have high interest rates, but the main commonality between them and store credit cards is that they all typically require excellent credit scores for approval.

When I worked in retail, people would grow frustrated when I asked them about our credit card application because hard inquiries make an impact on your overall credit score. This is especially true if you have lots of hard inquiries built up at once, although their effects fade over time, and they fall off your report after two years.

Credit Report Versatility

Just like your other investment portfolios, you want to have a diverse range of credit lines showing responsible use so that lenders know that they can rely on you. This means that you should have some credit cards, some loans, and other types of credit to get a diverse report. It's incredibly easy to diversify your credit history due to the increase in types of accounts that you can open.

For example, there are some installment loans that you are essentially paying yourself for. These will start with amounts like $500, and you get that $500 back after you have paid it off. Not only is this great for saving, but these payments look incredible on your credit report! It all depends on your needs; think about your monthly budget, your monthly bills, and your bigger-picture goals, such as buying a house or a car. How would these various credit lines help you get a car or home loan when you're ready?

Staying Responsible

Many people have a hard time remaining responsible with their credit because it feels different compared to the money that comes out of their checking account. They feel like it's a free opportunity to impulse spend, splurging to the tune of hundreds of dollars on things like expensive clothes they don't need. This can be especially tempting if their credit cards come with intriguing benefits like purchase discounts.

It's easy to forget that the idea behind building a good credit score is to be seen as trustworthy by lenders. I recommend that you keep your credit card utilization under 30% every month. Keeping it lower than that is even better, but sometimes 30% provides some realistic cushioning for things like unforeseen expenses. If your credit limit is higher, the 30% will look much different than if you had a secured credit card with a $200 limit. It's all about what you can afford to pay back.

The biggest tip I could give you for credit responsibility is remembering to make your minimum payment on time. Many credit cards only expect payments as low as $25, and they remind you in advance when your upcoming payment is due. You can even set reminders on your phone if you don't trust yourself enough to remember based on those contributors alone. Your credit score is impacted drastically by the average percentage of on-time payments that you make. If it falls below 90%, your score will significantly decrease. The amount of open, revolving accounts that you own will contribute to this factor. If you have more revolving accounts that you are continuously paying on time, you will likely have a higher average for your on-time payment percentage.

Checking Your Credit Score

These days, checking your credit score is as simple as downloading an app to your smartphone. Previously, many people believed the misconception that checking your credit score frequently would hurt it, occasionally with a sense of drama behind the idea. They thought that logging into a website and checking your score would automatically make you lose fifty points, despite having perfect payment history! This is not the case.

The ability to check your credit score from the convenience of your smartphone is both a smart business model and an incredibly helpful tool for people who previously had a hard time with credit.

There is a massive learning curve when it comes to understanding everything that goes into your credit report.

Generally, the concept of credit scores can be confusing; there are lots of numbers and data points to follow, and it can seem like one mistake can hinder your progress indefinitely. While mistakes can impact your credit score, there are things that you can do to rebuild it if you make a bad decision once or twice. After all, credit is like any other investment in that mistakes will happen eventually; you simply need to implement strong strategies into everything that you do with your finances.

Your credit report is comprised of several key factors that all make up your overall score:

> **Payments** — The amount of on-time payments that you make will impact your credit score the most. You want to make sure that you never fall below 99% of on-time payments because this can drastically lower your score. It's much more difficult to catch up on these payments once you've missed many of them. However, this can be combated by having multiple different lines of credit, so your on-time payments are coming from different sources. Just make sure that you don't bite off more than you can chew.

Credit Card Utilization — As a rule of thumb, it's good to keep your credit card utilization below 30%. Since every credit card limit is different, it's important to calculate what 30% would be in terms of your card specifically. For example, if you have a small line of credit that is $200, make sure you try to spend $60 at a time. I liked to use my secured credit cards for things like monthly Spotify payments. Small, recurring subscription services are a good idea to keep linked to your secured cards as long as you keep track of when this money will leave your account.

Derogatory Marks — Hopefully, you will never have to deal with derogatory marks. These include things like collections for unpaid debts or public records that negatively affect your credit report. Derogatory marks are hugely impactful to your credit score, and having even two on your report can hurt your score by more than 100 points. Be sure that you frequently check your credit report for any inaccurate derogatory marks or missed payments. You can directly dispute inaccurate findings from your credit report. Sometimes, as a worst-case scenario, you can request to negotiate with the creditor who holds a collection in your name. They occasionally offer pay-for-delete services, where you will pay the debt in full, and the derogatory mark falls off your account.

However, there is no way to ensure that creditors will keep their word. Additionally, not every creditor will agree to pay-for-delete negotiations. My advice is to keep your credit report clear of collections or public records altogether, but sometimes, mistakes happen, so it's beneficial to understand options.

Age of Credit History—This factor is often frustrating to new borrowers. It's like when you need to get a job, but you have no work experience. You're left to wonder who is going to give you the experience that you need for the job that you want. Your credit report looks at all your open accounts and averages the time that they have been open. This shows lenders that you have a long history of using credit responsibly. Thankfully, this does not impact your credit score that heavily. However, it's a good idea to keep it in mind when you are trying to build your credit score up from nothing.

Total Accounts—Similarly, the total number of revolving accounts, whether those are closed or open, does affect your score. This is one of the lowest-hitting contributing factors to your score, but I recommend keeping a decent number of revolving accounts open. This way, your range looks versatile. Generally, lenders like to see that you have used at least 11 accounts responsibly. That may seem like a large number now, but you'll find that it's rather easy to achieve. You might not enjoy the first credit card that you open, so you open another, and another, until you figure out what is right for you. All investments take time to feel "right" for individual investors, and personal credit lines are no exception to this rule.

Hard Inquiries — This is the part that scares a lot of newcomers. Many people have parents or other authority figures who have instilled a certain level of fear into them when it comes to applying for new credit lines. I do agree that it's important to keep your inquiries at a minimum, generally staying below five at a time, but I don't think that you should fear applying for new credit. On one hand, hard inquiries stay on your report for two years. That is a long time, but it's not the seven years that derogatory marks stay. On the other hand, hard inquiries have the lowest impact on your credit score out of all the categories we have discussed in this section. As a result, I suggest not going overboard on your applications when you look for your first line of credit, but don't worry that applying for too many accidentally will hinder your chances of having a good credit score.

Ultimately, it is possible for anybody to uphold the credit score that they desire. It will take time, as do all investments, but it is an aspect of your investment portfolio that should be considered heavily. Your credit score affects your ability to take out home loans, buy high-ticket items such as cars and electronics on installment plans, and more.

Your responsible use of credit now will make your life in your twenties much, much easier. When I was a teenager, I did not fully grasp the weight that my credit score would have on the rest of my life. I needed a lot of dental work done in my mid-twenties. These procedures are costly, so I needed a way to finance them. Most dentists offer financing options for their patients because of how important your teeth are to your wellbeing. So, as the date of my procedure drew nearer, I sat down and got very serious about the credit score that I currently had because it needed a ton of improvement.

I was able to change it by two hundred points in one month. If I didn't have internet resources, help from friends, and multiple sources of income, this wouldn't have been possible. However, I've dedicated much of my life to my journey towards financial freedom. It was, as you could imagine, freeing. I'm so glad that I was able to turn my credit score around, despite not really being great about using credit responsibly as a younger adult. Change is always possible in every aspect of your life. It's important to remember that you have control over these things so that you can live the lifestyle you truly desire.

CHAPTER SEVEN

RISK VS. REWARD: KEYS TO MAKE YOUR BUCKETS OVERFLOW

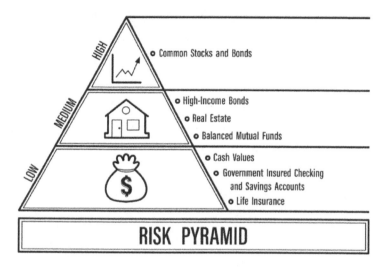

RISK PYRAMID

By now, you have a great understanding of the potential risk factors that could impact the quality of your investments. It may seem like a huge weight on your shoulders to keep up with everything. This shouldn't be the case; these days, there are ample resources available to keep you on track with your finances so that you never miss a beat.

I love the technological advancements that have been made in recent years because they add a layer of encouragement to new investors who may otherwise have been intimidated by all the information that they take in when they're learning. Whether you're reading an article on analyzing a stock chart, or you're trying to figure out if it's a good time to buy Bitcoin, a quick google search will usually ease most of your worries. Moreover, the reward that investors can expect is higher than ever because of the options that are at your disposal.

The fact that you can purchase stock from your smartphone is an absolutely mind-blowing development. There are still the same risks included in buying and trading stock that existed before, but this newfound accessibility ensures that more people are creating more opportunities for others. This forms a continuous cycle that ultimately benefits everyone. We've touched on the way that hype can affect your finances. People may persuade you to purchase a trendy new cryptocurrency, and if you're lucky, you'll get it when it's fresh, leading to a major reward in five years.

Unfortunately, many new investors do not appreciate the waiting period that comes with their investments. While you can make a good amount of money quickly with things like crypto and stock, you'll ultimately benefit the most from waiting an extended period as your investments simmer. This occasionally frustrating process will leave you thankful when you realize that you've made thousands just from being patient as your investments grow in value.

The Rule of 72

There are ways to project the outcome of all kinds of things. We have analyzed a few of them, briefly going over a few other formulas in previous chapters. The **Rule of 72** method allows us to project the value of an investment over time easily and quickly.

Sometimes, projection methods use over-complicated formulas that require at least one calculator and maybe an algebra class to figure out. This one, however, is incredibly simple. It estimates that if you divide your interest rate's percentage by 72, you can generate the number of years that will go by before your investment has reached double its original value.

The Formula

The Rule of 72 formula looks like this:

$$Years\ to\ Double = \frac{72}{Interest\ Rate\ (whole\ number - NOT\ a\ percentage)}$$

Why It Works

You can use the Rule of 72 on any compound interest investment. People use the Rule of 72 to calculate populations, rates for loans, and more. This formula helps investors see the reality of their investments. They can understand the speed at which they'll see a profit, which also allows them to become excited about watching their investment grow.

Investors love making money; this fact is a given! However, sometimes they have a difficult time being patient while their investments become more valuable. It's tempting to make an impulsive decision regarding investments when you don't think the time you have to wait is worth it. Investors who use the Rule of 72 get accurate projections for their investments, therefore providing them with more reasons to be patient with their projected results.

When You Are Patient

I believe that, above all else, patience truly is key. There is no amount of strategizing that you can utilize that will benefit you more than patience. For example, you may think that by following hourly stock market updates, you can cheat the system and reap quick rewards. While this is sometimes true, the level of inconsistencies will never be in your favor. I have learned this through so many personal examples.

When I first dabbled in stocks, I only bought small. I was so calculated with my every move. I followed news updates; I watched the charts — the whole 9 yards. But I was also only depositing small amounts at first, buying minimum amounts of shares because I wanted to slowly grow my portfolio. This strategy did work, but I was far too careful... until one moment when a spark of confidence brewed within me, and I took a risk.

Up until now, we've described risk as something that you want to avoid entirely. While it's true that you want to mitigate risk when it comes to your finances, risk is also an inevitable part of investing and life in general. Every successful investor, and every successful person, has taken at least one risk to get to where they are today or where they were at the peak of their career.

After I stopped being overly cautious about my stock portfolio, I realized that I could probably generate a good idea of the projected success of brands I knew well. I figured there was no reason to be pretentious about investing. I didn't need to select brands that were super underground and unheard of because I thought they'd be the next Apple in ten years.

Instead, I purchased stock in five of my most favorite brands. You don't need to know what those brands are to get the general idea. These were brands that were within my range of understanding. I didn't have to do extensive amounts of research to know that I would return a profit after a while. Additionally, I could use the Rule of 72 to see when my investment would double!

Five years went by after I purchased those stocks. At that point, they didn't just double, but they tripled in value by the time I was ready to sell them. I knew this because I trusted my gut and the Rule of 72 to guide me. I had faith in myself and the brands that I was investing in, so I knew that I would not regret those purchases later.

I didn't have to use expensive firms or advisors to make these decisions for me. Sometimes, using outside help has only hurt me in that sense. I'm quick to second-guess myself after even one person tells me that I should try something else or try something different. This has stopped me from seeing a lot of potential successes over the years.

A few months ago, I saw a TikTok video where a girl described an accidental success she had in terms of patience and investing. She first heard of DogeCoin when it was still a joke, nothing more than a would-be cryptocurrency based on a popular meme. She thought it was hilarious; the idea of crypto appealing to Gen Z specifically was mind-blowing to her, and she decided to participate in its very early stages.

What she didn't realize was that this is how many successful investors grow their earnings. Contrary to my story where I had faith built upon long-term relationships with brands, this method occasionally works, and when it does, it works wonders. The woman who told her hilarious story on TikTok purchased $11 worth of DogeCoin on her online brokerage account. She had bought a few stocks that year but wasn't a serious investor. By the time she made that TikTok, her $11 had turned into $5,000. She was grateful because she had some serious bills that she needed to pay, but she never expected a purchase she made as a joke to be that beneficial in the future.

Whether you are investing in brands you love or brands you want to love in the future, you must be patient to see the biggest possible rewards. If there is one thing that is certain, it is that you can generate a huge profit from the stock market and cryptocurrencies. Many people will tell you that you should strategize this way or that way, but you also must learn to trust your gut. If I could go back in time and put $11 into some DogeCoin back in 2017, knowing that I would be the proud owner of $5,000, I certainly would do so. Do not let today's impatience be tomorrow's loss.

When You Are Impatient

Of course, for every positive experience that investors at any skill level have had, there is at least one equal or worse negative experience that they use as a learning opportunity. As I have mentioned, failure should be a catalyst for your success. You cannot allow your failures to be setbacks; there are very few situations where failures are catastrophic enough to cause permanent damage.

Honestly, I do not believe that permanent damage exists, and most situations, especially financial ones, can be repaired. Of course, you must remain strategic. Failures will feel awful, naturally, because they are a blow to the ego above all else. I, for one, have certainly dug myself into a few holes that I thought I would never financially recover from.

On a less dramatic note, one of the very first times I purchased stock made me reevaluate my levels of patience and how I regulated them. I had a handful of shares in my portfolio, and it looked like there was an incredible surge in the market due to some hype that was generating around the companies I bought into. So, I sold them on a whim; I was enthralled by the quick change I had just earned. It was a few hundred dollars, and that seemed like a lot of money to me at the time. However, a few weeks later, the trading price for those stocks went up even higher, reminding me that if I had stayed in the game just a little bit longer, I could have reaped even bigger rewards.

I have faced similar instances of impatience with my credit cards. This is part of why I dedicate so much of my time to teaching financial literacy. It's not that I didn't have the resources at my disposal when I was irresponsible; it's that I was impatient and suffered because of that impatience.

When I got my first credit card, the limit was $300. Generally, I didn't use it to purchase much more than a small tank of gas or something from my Amazon wish list when I felt like I deserved a treat. One day, though, my favorite band announced a tour. Of course, I wanted to get tickets right away because I thought they would sell out instantly. I didn't have any money on my debit card, though, since I was in between checks from my retail job.

So, I thought there would be no harm in maxing out my credit card one time. I needed these tickets, and I would be devastated if they sold out before I could get them. And I always saw my favorite band at the very front of the general admission pit, which happened to be the most expensive kind of ticket that I could possibly get for that kind of event. Without thinking, I splurged on this ticket; it cost $298.88, just barely making the cut for my credit limit. I sighed, I cried, and I closed my mobile banking app, wondering how I was going to make it work.

I stayed up every night for those two weeks that I was in between checks, thinking of what I could do to get myself out of that situation. It was my fault; I couldn't blame anyone else for doing it, though I wasn't exactly mad that I was still going to see my favorite band again. But I also recognized the weight of the situation. I was now in debt for the first time ever, scrambling to pay it off, all because of my own impulses that I could not control.

As a result of my mistake, I owed about $150 in interest and bank fees. I had to use the next three checks paying this off in chunks, and eventually, my bank closed my account because I was incredibly irresponsible with it. This hurt my wallet and credit score briefly, but moreover, it impacted my standing at the bank with which I had previously had a golden relationship. While banks are not out to hurt you, they don't share the same human connection with you that a close friend or family member will have if you mess up once or twice. They trust you when you borrow from them, but that trust can be broken very easily. I didn't recognize how quickly your relationship with your bank can change when I was young, naïve, and desperately wanted some concert tickets.

No matter what you invest in, you must learn how to control your impulses. Any investment will show brilliant results if you are a little patient with it. Sometimes, you can see quick results in outlier cases like a surge in cryptocurrency. Of course, it is all circumstantial. Generally, though, you must remember to exercise patience in your investment. There will always be an emotional element to your finances, but your emotions cannot make your decisions for you.

Allowing them to do so will only dig you into deep financial holes, and you sometimes need a giant shovel to dig yourself out of those.

Diversification

Every great investor has a diverse portfolio. They don't put all their eggs in one basket, leaving lots of room for growth as markets change. This practice has been used since investment became a major player in people's finances, and it is especially important in our current financial climate. We are constantly conjuring up new ways to make investments and profit from them, so it may feel daunting keeping up with the latest trends.

Thankfully, you do not need to purchase every new form of cryptocurrency that generates hype for a few months to have a successful, diverse investment portfolio. There is a lot of beauty in diversifying your finances, and it is truly an art form that I believe every investor should master.

What Is Diversification?

In investment terms, **diversification** allows your exposure to any one asset type to be limited. This helps with market volatility since you would hopefully have a little bit of reach everywhere versus too much reach in just one. For example, only investing in stocks might result in a major loss if the market crashes. However, if you have some investment in stocks and some in cryptocurrency, you can think of your crypto, which may still be doing well, as a bit of leverage where your other assets might be lacking.

If you do stick to a niche, like stocks, you can still diversify your stock portfolio without venturing too far from it into new assets that you're less comfortable with. People purchase stock in brands they're familiar with. Let's assume that you purchased stock in a major retailer, one that is known around the world despite only being in the United States.

You live with the assumption that your stock will do well consistently because they are a reliable brand. One day, this retailer shocks the world by announcing their support for a political candidate who typically would go against each of their core values, which have been made public through marketing campaigns. The brand's fans are angered by this, so much so that sales drop significantly. There is a massive boycott that breaks out, costing this company millions. Their stock market chart drops to red status, leaving you and many others in a hole.

The key difference that separates you and these other investors is that you also bought stocks in other industries. These brands are completely unaffected by the PR nightmare that the major retailer has found themselves in. The brand in question will likely be facing the effects of this marketing mistake for a few years to come. You, however, understood the importance of diversifying your investment portfolio, so you dedicated much of your time to purchasing different assets. This allows you to rest easy, reaping the benefits of making smart investments.

Generally, good things take time, and they're worth waiting for. Unfortunately, some clichés are right, as much as we may like to roll our eyes at them. We can take the advice of great investors who have waited years to see the progress that they desire, but we can also take the advice of a novice investor who accidentally purchased a meme cryptocurrency and gathered a major reward because of her patience with it. Over time, you'll understand what diversification and patience mean for your specific portfolio as you grow passionate about different kinds of assets.

For me, I like always having several assets in my portfolio. I will purchase stock, crypto, and one new asset type at the start of every fiscal year. This keeps me learning; I do not want to grow stagnant in my investing and continue to revert to "old reliable" as a defense mechanism. While I have a few tried-and-true options that have withstood several otherwise crushing economic moments, I dabble in new assets because I have found massive successes that way.

My first big win was in an asset I normally never would have thought twice about. I was apprehensive about it since it was out of my comfort zone, but I made over $10,000 from it within a few months' time. It just goes to show that your comfort zone is not always so comfortable after all, and patience remains king.

CHAPTER EIGHT

ADVICE: WHERE TO LOOK AND WHAT TO TRUST

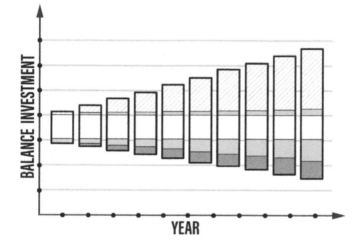

Gen Z is incredibly lucky because they have so many different avenues to choose from when it comes to investing. I am one to preach the wonders that come with accessibility in finances. I believe that when more people have access to things like brokerage accounts and financial firms, everyone benefits, and society can live sustainably.

Gone are the days where Wall Street was the only place where you could purchase stock, and even deeper in the past are the days where shareholders wear suits and ties to assert their dominance. You may have seen *The Wolf of Wall Street* and real-life copycats of Jordan Belfort try to return to the scene occasionally, but the world is completely different from the film's 1987 setting.

These days, you can get financial advice from your smartphone. This is incredible; most of the answers you seek are just a Google search away. Alternatively, accessibility paves the way for fakers to trick the naïve. You've probably heard the overused term "fake news," and its meaning has been warped to the point where many don't recognize the severity of the situation. "Fake news" isn't just limited to false or less-than-rosy depictions of political candidates. There are innumerous fake websites that exist solely to provide you with false information, especially because you are so young.

There are two main targets for false information online: the very old and the very young. The very old have not been exposed to this much technology until recently, so they must take extra steps to assimilate to it. The very young, like teenaged investors, are dealing with a much different beast: their own naiveté.

If you are reading this book, I assume that you are already ahead of the learning curve in many ways.

116

Don't let your ego tell you that you are immune to false information, though, especially when its current formats make it so difficult to escape. Most of us are on our social media feeds at all hours the day, but Twitter and Facebook are only a small fraction of the problem. However, limiting yourself to in-person resources would only hinder your progress as an investor and as a person. So, you must familiarize yourself with all potential outlets that you will encounter to avoid false information as much as you possibly can.

Reputable Resources

If your high school is or was anything like mine, they have likely taught you the importance of finding **reputable resources**. Mine gave us library courses on searching the internet and making sure you aren't looking at a fake site that's feeding you information that they think you want to hear or information that will scare you. Similarly, they taught us to even consider the news channels that we are watching. Human-made informational outlets will always operate with a certain level of bias. It's in our nature to push perspectives that benefit us and our agenda, but it's up to us to learn how to differentiate harmful bias from unharmful bias.

This is especially true in your finances; there are so many firms, fake loan schemes, and more that are predatory, only designed with the intention of digging you into a financial hole that takes years to climb out of. Research will help you, and you'll quickly begin to recognize red flags. Is this website trying to persuade you that their service can make you an exorbitant amount of money in a timeframe that seems extravagant? Are they fearmongering you? Learning how to spot these extremes will benefit you in the long haul.

Resources that are reputable in the financial sector typically include information that is directly from the source and do not include recycled variations of existing articles or websites. Personally, I am a fan of websites that do their best to minimize any opinions within their articles. As I mentioned, bias is human nature, but leaving as many opinionated statements as possible out of financial information is beneficial to investors because emotions play such a key role in our decisions. Try as we may to curb our emotions, we cannot eliminate our own bias, which often has us looking for information that we want to hear. I've fallen victim to this many times, and it's resulted in me making many irresponsible financial decisions when I could have done a little more research and avoided them completely.

It's safe to trust most government-run websites that deal with finances. I don't seek these out for advice most of the time, but they do answer a lot of my questions regarding legalities when I don't have another outlet to reach at the time. Try to avoid news channels for updates on your investments as a rule of thumb. CNN and Fox News are both incredibly biased even in their financial information, so I suggest looking elsewhere.

Alternatively, if you're looking for information from specific people, make sure that they have legitimate, provable credentials that authorize them to give you their advice. Financial advisors have a unique and lengthy set of requirements when it comes to what they can, cannot, and should not share. This helps you trust your intuition.

If a resource is reliable, you'll be able to tell based upon their credentials and the information that they're sharing. I trust other websites, like investment encyclopedias, but it just takes a bit of practice to differentiate between who is reliable and who is not. Ask yourself these questions while you analyze your resources for credibility:

- **Where did they get this information?** Was this taught to them in a professional or academic setting, and did they cite their sources?

- **Does the website look fraudulent?** Sometimes, red flags like significant grammar mistakes make it easy to see that a resource is illegitimate.
- **Does the information seem overly opinion-nated?** Minimizing confirmation bias helps you get the most out of what you're learning.

Over time, you'll find yourself going back to the same resources for information because you'll develop a trusting relationship with them. It's similar to choosing a bank; once you familiarize yourself with their rules and regulations, you're going to be in it for the long haul. If you find websites or other resources that you can trust to get financial advice from, you will likely return to them more than once after they've proven themselves to you.

Getting incorrect financial advice can drastically hinder your progress. Many people hire financial advisors, but there's plenty of free information available on the internet that you can use for casual circumstances. You shouldn't feel the need to pay an advisor for every financial question that arises. You can simply develop strong intuition for finding reputable resources instead.

"Pumpers" Are Not Your Friends

Jordan Belfort is the quintessential example of a "pumper." His role in *The Wolf of Wall Street* story perfectly exemplified pumpers' strategies to make a profit from your loss. While pumpers' plans occasionally work, allowing everyone to benefit from the hype, it is not your gains that they are concerned about.

They understand that they can recover from any losses due to hype-based investments, but people who operate on smaller-scale portfolios might not have that kind of luxury. All they care about is the potential to profit from the quick generation of increased prices for their stock. Usually, pumpers will have a high standing in the company they are shareholders in, providing them with a major advantage over everyone else. This is where the darker side of investment comes into play. You will, unfortunately, encounter greedy people who care more about their income than the people who are affected by their schemes.

Thankfully, technology has made it possible to spot pumpers more easily. This process is similar to investigating any resources that you use to find information. You must use your intuition; some pumpers are very clever, enticing you with carefully curated words or promises that make you believe that you're striking gold. Often, they use serious manipulation tactics to get what they want — and what they want is your money. You must remember this end goal when you encounter anybody who seems too good to be true.

Identifying a Pumper

Pumpers typically use the following tactics to get your attention:

- Cold calls that promise gains on your part when you engage with their schemes
- Influencers who ensure that you will make tons of money from their latest investment deal
- Targeting you based on your age—Since you are very young, they will likely promise that this will be a great opportunity for your beginners' portfolio without acknowledging the fact that there are great risks that come with that investment.

Avoiding Pumpers

I use the following techniques to avoid pumpers entirely:

- Reject calls from unknown numbers—iPhones will notify you if a scam is likely.

- Research all new investment opportunities that are promoted by social media influencers
- Recognizing that I'm still very young, especially in terms of investment opportunities, so many people could be taking advantage of me

Cryptocurrency Pumpers

Crypto is one of the most volatile investment opportunities that are currently available. You can purchase most of the popular cryptocurrencies via your PayPal account, making it extremely accessible. This is great since it makes it possible to generate a profit from it as an average person, even if you are not seriously engaged with investing.

However, if there is a serious drop in the crypto you invest in, you could find yourself at a loss. People like Elon Musk are known for promoting the latest cryptocurrencies so that they can generate massive amounts of hype towards it, ultimately leading people like you to suffer from a loss if it takes a large drop after the hype period is over. I won't disagree that these are good opportunities in the moment but use your better judgment before purchasing or selling your cryptocurrencies based on hype alone.

Financial Advisors

Traditionally, financial advisors have been most investors' go-to source for new information regarding their investments. These people are trained in this field so intensely that they can get seriously penalized for providing false information. Certified financial advisors are the most reputable resources that you can utilize, but not everybody can afford to go to an individual or a firm when they're starting out. Technology has made it possible to access several different kinds of financial advisors, leading new investors to avoid big mistakes due to receiving misinformation that they found elsewhere.

Human Advisors

Previously, before the internet, people had to visit other humans to get their financial advice. This practice seems ancient nowadays when you can simply Google a question and receive an answer in under a minute. Human advisors are wonderful because they will provide you with accurate information. They are at risk if they use shady business practices to generate a profit from your investments, for better or worse.

However, they are not as accessible as internet-based advisors, but they do try their best to be available to you when you need them. Similarly, many financial advisors have shifted their business structure to accommodate the market after COVID-19 hit. It's up to them to keep their businesses afloat, so many transitioned their firms onto online spaces. Several financial advisors offer tele-services such as Zoom meetings. It all depends on your preferences, but a human financial advisor will offer you "real conversations" that robot advisors sometimes cannot provide.

Robo-Advisors

Artificial Intelligence has become a great friend to us in recent years. It provides instant answers, constant communication, and more. Robo financial advisors are like other chatbots that you may see for places like the DMV. They are designed to offer quick support at a moment's notice, and they are usually accurate.

The downside to robo-advisors is that they might not always understand your question, leading to miscommunication and frustration. I use robo-advisors for easy yes-or-no situations versus long-form issues that may confuse them. Sometimes, trying to get an answer from a robo-advisor on a complex topic leads you to spend more time than you otherwise would have spent contacting another human.

Don't dismiss robo-advisors entirely, though. They can be a great source of information in several different situations. Keep in mind that their programming is geared to handle common questions. If someone else has experienced your issue or inquiry, robo-advisors will likely have an easy answer for you.

The Numbers

Math can be incredibly frustrating, even to the best of us. I excelled in most of my other subjects in school, but math was never my strong point. I struggled with it to the point where I only completed my basic courses in college, never venturing far from what I thought I could do. These were only self-perceived limitations, of course, but they greatly impacted my life as an investor when I began to take investing seriously. However, I found that doing math in terms of money made it that much easier. The math you learn in school is valuable, but it doesn't always make sense when there is a lack of real-world applications beyond potential career paths. Investment math always has a dollar sign involved at some point of the equation, leaving us "mathphobes" engaged because we recognize that these equations are designed to help us out.

Investment Calculators

While you continue to expand your portfolio, you'll want to keep up with factors like risk or growth via a visual representation. Sometimes, it's not possible to perfectly predict what your investment will look like in five years. It is good, though, to have a general idea. That way, you won't feel like you're going into an investment blind if you have a basic understanding of what it might look like for you in the future.

For example, if you want to purchase stock in a company, but you're not too sure of them just yet, you'll want to generate a projection of what you could expect realistically. **Investment calculators** are useful tools that can help you get a clear idea of several different aspects of your investments.

You can use an investment calculator to forecast growth over a certain period of time for several kinds of investments such as CDs, stocks, bonds, and real estate. As technology makes it easier for these calculators to be coded and distributed, more are becoming readily available. I believe that in five years, there will be an investment calculator online for virtually any form of investment.

I use investment calculators for higher-ticket investments such as real estate. This is especially true because real estate is something I still consider myself to be a novice in. I just started buying property within the past two years after my business began taking off, and the numbers became lost to me rather quickly. With the powerful investment calculators that I found online, I was able to ease this burden and organize my assets.

Basic Math

I was never great at math. It was my least favorite subject, and I consistently found myself putting minimal effort into every math class I took. It wasn't until my final math requirement in community college that I ended with an exceptional grade. The "A" I earned in that class was truly motivational, but I credit a lot of that effort to my newfound interest in investment.

As I began to grow more passionate about cleaning up my finances, I learned that I needed to have a better understanding of basic math to keep my financial life organized. If I couldn't properly handle certain basic skills, I would easily lose track of things as I gained more assets. This is especially true as the value of my assets increased. When I failed to understand basic math, larger numbers seemed very intimidating. This resulted in me limiting myself because I thought I couldn't handle the bigger numbers for the assets that I desired.

You don't have to commit to a math or business major in college to get a good understanding of the basic skills that you'll need for your investments. I only completed up to advanced algebra, which was the highest requirement for my major in English. Still, advanced algebra paved the way for the financial equations I would be doing on a regular basis. In this guide, we've gone over several of the formulas you can use to calculate your financial future. If you have ever entered variables into an equation and solved for them, you will be able to solve each equation that I have detailed in this guide.

I think it's important that we discuss math because it can be frustrating for many people. Again, it's important to note that I was the only one holding myself back for the first several years of my investment journey. I could have been handling thousands of dollars in assets, but I let fear limit me.

Investing sounds especially daunting if you factor in things like stock charts that just add to the overall confusion you will face when you're getting started. However, you have plenty of time to get to the advanced work. I recommend using digital calculators like Wolfram Alpha for certain equations when you have the formula but not the time or capacity to accurately solve for the variable. Calculators have helped me so much. Free tools have completely changed the game for novice investors and college students. Overall, it's important that you have rudimentary math skills to get by and expand upon them as you continue investing in more complex assets.

Carefully protecting your assets will help you in both short and long-term investments. I don't recommend spending lots of money solely for protection purposes because you can get most of these resources online for free or at a very low cost. If your needs are more complex, of course, this budget will change substantially. As you're starting out, it's important to minimize the pressure that you place upon yourself. You don't need the fanciest equipment to get the job done, but many places will try to sell you things you don't need, claiming that you'll see the best results if you exclusively use their products.

This is also true of other resources. Websites that offer specialized information are offering you a service, but there may be ulterior motives at play. Of course, when we are discussing investing, our primary concern is money. Often, when people discuss money, they forget the humanitarianism that is involved with the topic.

Many people grew up without a lot of money at their disposal, so when they discover investment as a viable means of financial growth, they are intimidated by these factors and occasionally get scammed by people who have poor intentions. Consider your own upbringing when you are seeking reputable information, both online and in person. Would someone want to take advantage of you because you are exceptionally wealthy or poor? Many forget that both sides of the spectrum are susceptible to harmful practices. If you have a lot of what someone else wants, they may go to extreme lengths to take it from you.

I don't want you to live with paranoia, though. Many people recognize the risk of being duped and look over their shoulders three times for every step they take. This paranoia sets them back. Any overwhelming fear is limiting because they could be spending that time getting their information someplace that doesn't throw up those red flags. Your fight-or-flight response will likely be on high when you're first learning how to deal with larger sums of money, especially if you're not used to it. The same is true if your parents or guardians had a strict mindset when it came to finances.

It's up to you to take lessons from family or friends and use them as a positive catalyst for change. You are here for your own growth; you do not need their past mistakes to define your future ones, or their past successes to define your current ones. Your path is entirely yours, and what you make of it depends on your effort, time, and critical-thinking skills.

Money is wonderful in that it's possible for anyone to take nothing and turn it into something. However, many people are not given the resources to do so, leaving most people behind the learning curve. Since you're already ahead just by reading this, you know that you can overcome the fears that are often created by narrow beliefs and generational roadblocks.

Financial freedom takes time to achieve, but the mountain in the way is not unsurmountable. I remember when it felt like the biggest hurdle I would ever have to leap over, which was actually not too long ago. I think it's important to emphasize the fact that I am still learning, even with my expertise in my front pocket guiding me. If I'd let fear hold me back or let any losses prevent me from continuing my efforts, I would not be writing this guide to help teens find their way through investment. Understanding that the purpose was greater than seeing a few more commas in my bank account was the first step, and I have been able to grow so much since then.

CONCLUSION

WHERE YOU ARE VERSUS WHERE YOU STARTED

I want you to think back to what you knew when you began reading this guide. I imagine you at least knew that you wanted to be ahead of the learning curve, allowing your insight into investing to guide you through college and beyond.

As graduation approaches, it's crucial that you encourage your growth without putting too much pressure on yourself to know everything right away. You already knew more than I did about investing when I was your age. That's right—you have an advantage even over the person who taught you all that you now know from reading this book. The mentor always eventually becomes the mentee, and I think that's the best part of circulative knowledge. I can pass on to you what I wish I'd known at your age, allowing you to go even farther than I have on your journey to reach your goals.

Throughout the course of this book, you have learned:

- Basics regarding investing, including what forms of investing are available to you
- How to open a bank account and keep your assets safe
- What can make your assets grow
- What can diminish your assets
- Potential risk factors when you are considering investments
- The importance of stocks and the basics for navigating the stock market
- Protecting yourself and your investments from harmful, false information
- Where to get credible information that ultimately helps you organize your assets and grow your wealth

I believe that knowledge is an asset in and of itself. While you focus on material assets, don't forget to focus on continuing growth in terms of knowledge. There's always more to learn; investing is just like any other skill, hobby, or job. Thinking that you know everything because you've reached a specific goal will only lead to stagnation. Considering the forward movement that investments are making due to technology, it's crucial to consistently keep yourself updated with what's trending, even though you don't want to make all your financial decisions based upon current trends. Be informed but remain cautious.

The current and future generations of professional investors have the task of separating the way they view trends that they see elsewhere from the information that's available in their financial lives. While technology is a blessing that continuously lets us grow more innovative, it also has shortened the shelf lives of all trends in any possible niche.

For example, the rise in cryptocurrency has made it possible for people to start their investment portfolio from their PayPal accounts, but it also relies a lot on hype-based growth. Elon Musk helped popularize the cryptocurrency DogeCoin, which started off as a joke that got its name from a meme. Many other online influencers followed in his footsteps, encouraging their audiences to make financial decisions. Most of these influencers didn't have completely selfish intentions, but if DogeCoin suddenly tanked, their viewers would be resentful towards them because they did their job — they influenced them.

With that being said, the fact that you have this guide puts you at an advantage compared to most of your peers. I encourage you to share this knowledge with your friends. Having open conversations about finances is difficult for most people, but it can be life changing if you're encouraging your peers to make healthy decisions. I recommend talking about these things with people you're close to, not acquaintances, because it may feel like you're overstepping if you lack a comprehensive understanding of their situation.

Just as you would with any other book that you've read, tell them you've read this one. Everybody starts somewhere, and some people don't take the leap because they don't know where to look for what they need to get things going. This is especially true if you're not yet 18. A lot of financial opportunities feel closed off before you graduate high school. That may seem frustrating right now because you just want to see the results right away, but good things take time. My credit score, for instance, didn't see substantial growth until my mid-twenties — and it's still going strong.

If you're not yet 18, but you want to get started in investing, I recommend that you consider this year to be your research phase. You've already completed step one by reading this guide, so give yourself a pat on the back! From here, you can begin to take small steps towards getting a new bank account, beginning your savings account, and potentially even getting your first job.

My first job felt so liberating. Even though it was short lived, I learned so much about myself. It taught me the basics about saving up for things that I wanted because my parents stopped giving me a weekly allowance as soon as I was earning my own money. This felt like a punishment when they first did it, and I was rather dramatic about the whole thing. In retrospect, it was certainly for my own good. Usually, your parents or guardians will want what's best for you.

They're also a great place to start in terms of financial advice, especially as you're starting out. I have mentioned, and want to emphasize, that it's important to learn from them without basing your entire self-worth on your parents' gains or losses. Many people get their sense of self-worth based on their finances, so it's important to find a balance early on to avoid falling into that trap.

You can do many amazing things that are irrelevant to how well your stocks are doing or how much money you have in your checking account. However, having financial freedom can feel like a massive victory. It certainly was for me. It wasn't something that felt easily accessible due to the experiences of others that I had seen. We were well off, certainly, but it still felt like my parents were restricting themselves in many ways, so I decided to change that.

My first massive victory was when I purchased my own car. I was always terrified of driving, so the fact that I even wanted to gain the ability to drive was shocking to most people who knew me. I was always picking up rides from other people, but I grew tired of relying on others to get me where I needed to go. I also didn't hesitate to get the car I wanted instead of aiming lower because it felt "realistic." Being unsatisfied with the car

I owned would just make me want to drive it less, keeping me in the same cycle of relying on others to get what I wanted.

The same goes for your finances. Others can help guide you to where you need to be, but the decisions are ultimately yours. Only you can call the shots on which stocks to buy, or which cryptocurrencies you'd like to trade, or which real estate properties you want to purchase. Your preferences will be different from the next person's, just like anything else.

Additionally, the people close to you should be open to talking about these things when you get scared or frustrated. Emotional investing is totally a thing, but it shouldn't be a complete hindrance to your progress. Now, it's time to take your training wheels off and hit the ground running. You've got all the tools you need, and before you know it, you will be financially free and living your best life.

Made in the USA
Las Vegas, NV
16 December 2021

37937463R00079